THE TRAVELER'S EDGE

THE TRAVELER'S EDGE

HOW TO USE TRAVEL AS YOUR UNFAIR ADVANTAGE IN BUSINESS AND LIFE

GEORGE MEGRE

EDITED BY IYA MEGRE

NEW DEGREE PRESS

THE TRAVELER'S EDGE

How to Use Travel as Your Unfair Advantage in Business and Life

ISBN   978-1-64137-202-2   *Paperback*

            978-1-64137-203-9   *Ebook*

For Guram and Grandpa.

TRAVEL AGENDA

POINT OF DEPARTURE

———

How do you succeed today?

An endless amount of research and personal opinions will give you a variety of answers.

But my answer is simple and straightforward.

Travel.
Travel for pleasure.
Travel for work.
Travel on a whim.
Travel with a great deal of planning.
Travel for long trips.
Travel for short visits.

Travel in your home country or city.

Travel as far away as you can get.

But mostly just travel, and then travel some more.

Some people may argue that only *certain* travel counts or is valuable or should be encouraged. Frankly, I'm less concerned with where or how you travel; I just want you to try to travel, because I'm convinced that the single best way for you to increase your chances of happiness and success comes from developing a great proclivity for travel.

How do I know? Well, partly from my own experiences, which have shown me that my growth has been fostered through travel. But you don't have to take just my word for it: my belief has been reinforced time and again from studying and speaking to some of the most successful people from all walks of life.

**

"This is it... my last hurrah."

I remember the thought crossing my mind as I pressed "buy" on an open-ended ticket to Thailand. I was going to be traveling alone for the first time in my life, so I had no idea whether I would want to come back in a week or brave staying away for the full month that I was aiming for. I was

22 years old and I had just spent the previous three months traveling across the globe for the best summer of my life (at that point).

Freshly graduated and with less than a month and a half before I was to start my first post-college job, I thought that this trip would be the last of my extensive travel. I believed what everyone tells you about life after college: decades of grinding away at your desk, hoping that the odd work trip will send you somewhere interesting and give you enough time to leave the airport hotel, or scrimping together your savings and your vacation days for the occasional exotic vacation. Freedom was for the foolhardy youths; real adults squash their travel bugs and make do with stay-cations.

I was wrong.

My thirst to traverse the globe would only grow stronger in the years to come. In the decade since that moment, I've done more travel than I had ever imagined—and I've learned more lasting and impactful lessons from those journeys than I ever did in a classroom or in a board meeting.

Mark Twain said, "Travel is fatal to prejudice, bigotry, and narrow-mindedness, and many of our people need it sorely on these accounts. Broad, wholesome, charitable views of men and things cannot be acquired by vegetating in one little corner of the earth all one's lifetime." And Mark Twain lived in a time when it took weeks on a miserable boat to travel a few thousand miles; I think he would be very disappointed to see people today fail to take advantage of what we can see and do.

I am a firm believer that we are the sum of our experiences, and when I look back at those memories the most vivid ones are those of travel.

Most of us have approached travel incorrectly. While there is nothing wrong with vacationing just to turn your mind off and escape the humdrum of daily life, we can do so much more—things that no generation before us could. Travel can be a tool to learn, to grow, and to bring out the best version of you. And traveling won't just make you more interesting than the next person at the cocktail party: it can sharpen your business acumen, make new connections internal and external, and help you get ahead in any industry.

My hope is you'll read *The Traveler's Edge* and come away with the following insight:

Travel is—or can be—your unfair advantage in life.

Before I started working on this book, I hoped that was true— if only to justify my love of travel and all those hours I've spent on planes, trains, and automobiles. But after combing through the research and interviewing some incredibly successful individuals about the core lessons of mindful and intentional travel, I'm convinced.

Travel *should* be your unfair advantage in life.

And in this book, I'll demonstrate how others have leveraged travel to get ahead and guide you on how you can do the same.

Of course, there will be naysayers. Some people may say:

- *I don't have the time to travel.* I say, "Travel doesn't have to take weeks or months, and you don't have to do it regularly to see results. An evening out here, a long weekend there, or just sporadic trips every other year—any amount is good, if your attitude is right."
- *I don't have the money to travel.* I say, "You can travel within your own city, on whatever budget you can manage, and *still* get all the benefits of traveling."
- *I'm scared to travel and have heard bad things.* I say, "Travel is safer now than ever before, but it's okay to feel nervous. Bring a friend, do some research, and you can find adventure while still feeling safe."
- *I don't like to travel.* I say, "You might be doing it wrong. But, if you're sure, you have my blessing to give this book to someone who does."

The Traveler's Edge is a tool for your personal development.

For many of you, this book might serve as a justification for doing something you *already* love to do. And that's fantastic—especially if it makes you do more of it.

For others, this book may introduce something new to your life as you recognize that travel—particularly travel done mindfully and intentionally—can be more powerful than getting a graduate degree, reading dozens of books, or hiring a life coach.

And for still others of you, this may help you kick-start that itch you have to travel, or add a new dimension to what you previously thought travel was for.

**

How do we become more successful in our lives and our careers? Again, it's a big question with a lot of answers. I found that one of the most compelling, well researched, and comprehensive collections of guidance for success was assembled by Leon Ho, the Founder and CEO of Lifehack (which is itself a community dedicated to individuals seeking self-improvement). After researching thousands of books, articles, and findings, he summarized his work into thirteen core principles to succeed:

1. Think big.
2. Find what you love to do and do it.
3. Learn how to balance life.
4. Do not be afraid of failure.
5. Have an unwavering resolution to succeed.
6. Be a person of action.
7. Avoid conflicts.
8. Don't be afraid of introducing new ideas.
9. Believe in your capacity to succeed.
10. Always maintain a positive mental attitude.
11. Don't let discouragement stop you from pressing on.
12. Be willing to work hard.
13. Be brave enough to follow your intuition.

It's tough to take issue with any of the principles; they certainly resonate and feel like things we *should* do to succeed.

But after reading Leon's strategies (and hundreds of others similar success frameworks), I was left with the same question: How? How do you get from here to there?

My quest through the research for this book was to confirm what my gut told me: the *how* is through mindful and intentional travel. And I feel stronger in that belief now than I did at the beginning of my journey.

The Traveler's Edge is designed to showcase how travel can help you to:

1. Spark your creativity.
2. Expand your perspective.
3. Increase your confidence.
4. Acquire new skills.
5. Improve your wellness.
6. Build your network.
7. Deepen your spirituality.

(And it will outline how to do each of these things whether you're traveling for study, work or leisure—even if you're traveling in your own backyard.)

There is a multitude of scientific studies to back up these claims—all of which I will dive into later in the book—but all of this is intuitive and only makes more sense the more you think about it. It makes sense that your creativity grows when you are exploring new environments and your brain reacts to new inputs. It makes sense that you will gain perspective when you see different parts of the world and experience it as other people do. It makes sense that you will gain confidence the more you step away from your safety net and find success outside of your routine. It makes sense that you will be healthier physically and mentally when you spend your time exploring instead of shuttling between your desk and your bed. It makes sense that you will find your personal world has gotten bigger when you expose yourself to more people and places. And it makes sense that you'll feel more spiritually connected when you open yourself up to the world at large.

Now, it's important to note that I'm encouraging *mindful* and *intentional* travel as a tool to increase your success in your career and your life.

This means that travel can be mindless and without intention. That doesn't make it bad travel *per se*, just not necessarily the travel that'll improve your chances of success. Think of that travel as the traditional business trip where you never step outside the work bubble (you go from flight to cab to hotel brand to office and back). It's travel, but it's also not travel at all—more like the same old job in front of a green screen showing new backdrops. The same can be said of a vacation at a resort, or a vacation spent doing a narrow band of tourist-friendly activities. These trips can be relaxing and enjoyable, but again may not be intentional or mindful—the travel equivalent of going to a restaurant and ordering the same dish you cook at home.

Travel can be an advantage when it's more than just a "vacation."

The majority of people view travel as a reward for their hard work or a way to get away from the stresses of "the real world." I believe that travel *is* the real world. Many people will have travel to some country or another on their "bucket list"—a phrase that creates a sense of nebulousness and lack of immediacy. I contend that you should move travel from your "bucket list" to the top of your "to-do list."

I will state it outright: it is a mistake to hold off on that life-changing trip that you've been dreaming about. The earlier you travel the better.

If you had the option to make yourself a better person, would you wait until later in your life to do it? There is a reason people have thirteen or more years of education at the start of their lives; what would be the benefit of waiting to learn *later*? The earlier you learn a skill, the better; and travel teaches you countless valuable skills.

The experiences that travel brings will not only help you grow as an individual, but also help you build a more fulfilling and financially stable life for yourself. It is an investment in your present and future. And it is never too early or too late to go out into the world because each time you do it may bring new lessons.

Some folks say that all they need is a weekend away to feel their creative juices flowing. Some contend that you need long-term travel, or to relocate entirely, in order to feel the benefit. Others believe that you need to challenge yourself. Most would agree that a weekend of partying in Cancun won't do anything other than kill some brain cells and make your liver want to pack its bags for its own vacation. I am here to tell you that any and all those things can be true.

Like most things in life, the benefits from travel depend on entirely how present you are in your situation, what you choose to do, and how you choose to do it. If you are open to trying new things and being out of your element, then creativity and inspiration are not far behind. Even if you are not, I firmly believe that with enough time, traveling can help you grow into that person.

This book is a collection of stories and life lessons from successful individuals; some of them I know personally, or have long been aware of, and others I've only discovered through research for this book. Some of their names will sound very familiar, and others are complete strangers. All of these people share a common thread.

They've all changed—for the better—because of travel.

**

Before we jet off on this journey, a little about me.

I'm George and I live in New York.

I'm originally from Georgia. (No, this is not the Georgia that you are thinking of.) I'm from the Republic of Georgia. (No, I am not making up a country just because my name is George.) Considering it has a population of fewer than four million people, it's no surprise that most have never heard of it; in fact, the state of Georgia has nearly three times as many people as the country.

I can't say exactly when my passion for travel started, but I can say that it is all thanks to my mother. She spent the majority of her life behind the Iron Curtain of the Soviet Union. Not only was travel restricted, but the exchange of information was even filtered through the communist propaganda machine. Fortunately for her and the rest of my family, we were able to immigrate to the United States of America in May of 1993, when I was eight years old. This was two full years following the collapse of the Soviet Union, so you can imagine the difficulty of leaving the country.

Once we were out, it was like the flood gates had opened. My mom wanted to go everywhere, and she refused to go anywhere without taking her family (my father, my sister, and me). She had a lifetime of experiences to make up for, so she took every opportunity to go somewhere new and do something different. Whether nature or nurture, my passion was born from her. I never feel quite as alive as I do when I am planning my next adventure, and I imagine many of you reading feel the same way—or want to. After all, you chose to pick up this book.

I've been to approximately 80 countries and territories (the exact figure varies based on whose definition of statehood you follow) around the globe, and I don't intend to slow down anytime soon. In fact, I hope to spend more time in many of the places I've already been to deepen my connection to and understanding of the environment. While the majority of my travel has been for leisure, I've also spent a significant amount of time traveling for academic purposes and work as well.

But the real question is: why should you listen to me?

Well, you shouldn't. At least, you shouldn't listen to *only* me. *The Traveler's Edge* is a collection of thoughts I have assembled from others—including people a lot more successful and famous than me—so you can make the most out of our collective wisdom.

Lucky for you, you're not in Soviet Russia, so you have lots and lots of wonderful choices! I still remember how restricted everything was back then, which is why I've spent so much effort to talk to as many people as possible and to find the most useful research out there. Hopefully you, reading this book, can take full advantage of the freedom that you have before you.

I recognize how valuable your time is. From the bottom of my heart, thank you for taking the time to read this book. I sincerely hope that what you learn here inspires you and pays dividends that far outweigh the investment you've made.

Bon voyage!

MAP KEY

———

How to Navigate

What do you want out of this book?

If you know the answer to this question already, then you're ahead of the game! If not, now is your chance to give it some thought. As with many journeys, you have a higher chance of success if you know your destination.

If you are unsure of your goal, or have many of them, don't fret! *The Traveler's Edge* was written to cover a very wide range of topics, so regardless of who you are or where you are in life, we can discover your trajectory together.

Orientation

Is this a book about travel, a self-help book, or a guidebook?

Yes! All of the above. Because this book urges you to consider how travel can improve your life, it has been designed to mimic a travel guide—with your success and growth as the destination. As such, the book is intended to be used actively on your transformational journey.

The Traveler's Edge has three sections: The Traveler's Mind, The Traveler's Tool Set, and Means of Travel. The first two parts demonstrate how you can use travel to level yourself up in seven specific aspects. The final section considers the different purposes that you can travel for (study, work, leisure, or even in your own backyard) and provides a tactical guide to each.

The chapters, called "Destinations", each focus on a particular aspect of your life that can be enhanced by travel. The structure within each destination chapter is as follows:

- First, the **Roadmap** offers a quick introduction to each topic.
- Next, you'll visit the **Top Sights**, which are stories, research, and other helpful information related to the topic.
  - Don't forget your **Souvenirs**, which are the main takeaways from each story.

- After you've toured the sights, you'll read up on **Getting Around**. This is a summary of what we learned in the chapter, extra tidbits, and some thoughts on how to apply it all to your own life.
- Finally, we bring it all together with a **Suggested Itinerary**. These are action steps based on what you've learned about each destination. This is the section that you should come back to most often to figure out how to make your own way.

Travel Advisory

Travel is different for everyone, so I cannot guarantee that following these directions will give you the exact outcome you're looking for. But I do promise that these suggestions can serve as great first steps to your ultimate goal. Besides, what's a little risk in the face of all that reward?

Wayfinding

What's the best way to get around?

If you are a nerd like me who enjoys reading from cover to cover, then *The Traveler's Edge* is perfect for you. But some people prefer to skim and jump around, and others want to return to their favorite themes and stories quickly. For you,

I've made sure to make each chapter of this book able to stand on its own, and I've tried to signpost important points for ease of reference.

In short, you have to work pretty hard to get lost in here. And if you're just wandering, I hope you'll be pleasantly surprised by what you find.

Before You Go

What should I watch out for?

The Traveler's Edge is full of stories of real people who have been changed by their travels. Many of these people may be familiar to you, and some of them won't be, because famous people are not the only ones with stories worth telling. But I want to make clear that by relating one particular story about an individual, I do not mean to condone their views or actions outside of the story as set down here. People are complicated, and no one is perfect. If you're not a fan of Starbucks or if you think consultants have a terrible job, that's okay! You are entitled to your opinion, and I have one too. This book won't try to sell you coffee or mold you into one specific type of person.

That said, I believe you can still learn from people's stories, even if you don't like or agree with them on anything else.

Please keep that in mind before you decide to skip a story, and its accompanying lessons, just because it's about your least favorite Beatle. (I may be biased because we share a name.)

Ready, Set…

Anything else I need to know?

Don't just read… do! Take action! I would rather you follow the action steps at the end of a single chapter than read the whole book but do nothing I suggest.

I was once told to read as if you are having an argument with the author. I'm down; are you? Please feel free to use your pens, pencils, and highlighters vigorously. If something is really helpful or pertinent, then mark it down. If you disagree with something, go ahead and yell at me by writing in capital letters in the margins. Who knows? Maybe somewhere out there, I will hear you, get a headache, and try to make myself feel better by taking another vacation.

So, I think that's everything. All set?

Go!

PLANNING YOUR TRIP

———

"The pleasure we derive from journeys is perhaps dependent more on the mindset with which we travel than on the destination we travel to."

—ALAIN DE BOTTON, *THE ART OF TRAVEL*

Before we embark on our journey, let's take a step back to consider a wider view on the significance of travel.

The travel industry isn't just about vacations and work trips. As Tom Lowry, the Managing Editor for Skift (a platform that provides news, research, and marketing to travel businesses), put it: "Travel has the first window, in terms of business, on world events and economic trends… It serves as a proxy for other businesses because travel is the first to get hit or exposed to [economic downturns]. So from that point of view, travel can tell a broader business and economic story." In the same vein, travel is of vital importance to local and global markets: the health of a community's, or country's, travel industry is an early indicator of its economic health as a whole.

In this section, we will look at the state of the travel industry, discuss why and how you should travel, and finally examine the concepts that will be used throughout this book.

The Current State of Travel

Look at almost any wish list and you'll see travel at the top of it. Look at any survey of biggest regrets and you'll see not having traveled (or traveled more) near the top as well. For example, a recent American Express survey reported that 88% of Americans put "traveling to new places" as the number one item on their bucket lists, above having children and pursuing a passion. Travel is one of the few universal desires that we share. After all, who wouldn't want to see what lies beyond their boundaries? Who doesn't dream of adventure?

Since the turn of the century, global international tourism revenue has nearly tripled, resulting in an industry that generates over $1.3 trillion annually (and growing). Add domestic tourism and this figure goes up to nearly $2.6 trillion.

In addition, as it has grown by leaps and bounds, so has travel become more accessible to more people. People are now traveling to destinations that they would only have had the opportunity to see in photos and television just a few decades ago.

Travel is no longer exclusively for the wealthy. Yes, airfare and hotel prices as a whole may have risen, but more options—and more affordable options—mean that, with a little bit of sweat and ingenuity, nearly anyone can afford to go somewhere on their budget. The internet allows us to have much more transparency on lodging and flight options and there is no end to the number of travel hack websites that can get you a round-trip ticket to Europe for less than a one-way to Seattle. Even deal sites like Groupon now sell vacation packages at reduced prices. And if you blow all your money getting there, sites like CouchSurfing allow you to sleep on a stranger's couch for free. So while some costs may have increased, the options available to you have dramatically grown as well, and the barriers to this information have been virtually eliminated—meaning you don't need a travel agent, just an internet browser and the willingness to do a little shopping around.

All in all, it's more than likely you already have everything you need to get going: the desire to travel and the means to do it. But let's make sure you're doing it right.

Why Should You Travel?

Have you heard of "the Easterlin Paradox"? If you're familiar with the phrase "money doesn't buy happiness," you're
most of the way there. The Easterlin Paradox tells us that
happiness varies directly with income both among and
within nations, but over time happiness *does not* trend
upward as income continues to grow. Basically, the more
money you make, the happier you are—*up to a certain
point*. Once you reach a certain critical point where your
needs are met, increasing your income alone does not affect
your happiness.

For example, a minimum-wage worker at Walmart will
probably see a direct positive impact on their life with
a raise of even a dollar or two. At the lowest levels of income,
it's hard to handle basic necessities like rent, transportation
costs, and groceries (let alone splurge on a trip to Disn-
eyland). Maybe with a raise, that worker can lease a car
instead of having to wait for the bus every morning. But
Walmart's CEO probably would not see the same change in
his life for a few dollars an hour, or even an extra million
on top of his $23 million compensation. Sure, the amount
in question is much bigger, but the money's marginal effect
on his life—and happiness—is nonexistent. Maybe he'll
buy a new car, or even upgrade an existing car to something nice and impractical like a Ferrari, but it's not like
he doesn't already have the means to get from Point A to

Point B. His life has not been qualitatively improved in any tangible way. Any happiness he gets from the novelty will be short-lived—about as long as it takes for a Bugatti to come speeding by.

The Easterlin Paradox was originally conceived in 1974 by Richard Easterlin, a professor of economics at the University of Pennsylvania. Professor Easterlin used data from 1946 to 1970, all from the United States. Since then, researchers have looked at data from 1.7 million people and across 164 countries. As recently as 2018, their findings confirmed the same point: after a certain incremental point, money just won't buy happiness.

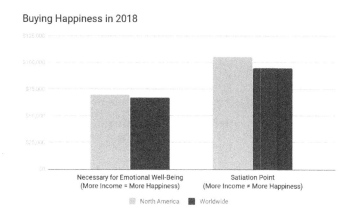

Buying Happiness in 2018

So, if money won't do it, what will? And what *should* you do with your money?

Travel. Duh. Experiences can buy you happiness where money can't. (And, luckily, money can often buy you travel.)

Thomas Gilovich, a psychology professor at Cornell who spent decades researching the topic, agrees: "Your experiences connect you to other people in ways that your material goods don't, and that continues to be a gift that keeps on giving. And so it turns out—and a lot of research has shown this—that even though the experience comes and goes possibly in a flash, it lives on psychologically and provides more enduring satisfaction and enjoyment."

This book has a particular focus geared toward how travel can help you get ahead in your career. But I also want you to remember that the journey itself is its own reward.

How Should You Travel?

Today, one of the fastest-growing segments within the travel industry is experiential travel. This means that you want to focus on experiencing a particular place by meaningfully engaging with its history, people, culture, food, and environment. As you may have noticed, this is pretty broad— experiential travel can be something as simple as having dinner with a local family to trekking across the desert with a nomadic tribe. No matter how large or small your action, you are forging a deeper connection than you would be sitting by a pool with your phone in one hand and a coconut full of sugary alcohol in the other.

In one 2017 survey, 65% of travelers said that they preferred "experiencing something new" to "feeling rested and recharged." (This brings to mind the old saying, "A change is as good as a rest.") Many companies have taken notice: major sites like Airbnb have begun to offer travel "Experiences"—everything from a graffiti tour to a wolf encounter.

Of course, there's nothing wrong with going on a vacation to recharge your batteries. It's probably the most common form of travel, and I have no desire to take it away from the people that need and value it. But if you're going to spend the time and effort to travel, consider finding time to do something more meaningful. If your only goal is to get away from work or pesky family members, you can achieve similar results booking a hotel room ten minutes from where you live and telling everyone that you've elected to recreate your own personal season of *Survivor*. (Jeff Probst will be played by your handsomest pillow.)

Just as it's a pretty big waste of time and money to go to an expensive private university for four years of binge-drinking and binge-watching, it can be a waste to travel to a foreign place and spend the trip walking from hotel pool to hotel restaurant. You don't have to go so far as to spend your entire vacation volunteering—although volunteer tourism *is* a fantastic way to spur personal growth. But if you make it all the way to Dubrovnik, maybe you visit a restaurant outside the tourist center, even if it means there's no convenient English-language menu. If you're island-hopping in the Caribbean, maybe you charter a boat operated by a local and treat the captain to a beer and chat about his life. These are not big asks, but can make all the difference between checking out of the everyday and checking into something amazing.

This book has dual purposes. The first purpose is simple: to make you travel more. The second is equally important, but a little more nuanced: to make you more aware, not only while traveling but in everything that you do, so that you can make the most of the journey of your life.

Throughout the book you will read about travel that is mindful, intentional, and other similar adjectives. Sometimes, the sentiment behind these adjectives is interchangeable, but I've broken out my definition of the two most important below. These definitions are broad; it's up to you how far you want to go with these concepts.

Mindful travel asks you to be more present in the moment. You don't have to do any specific activity, but whatever it is, think on what you've done, are doing, or are about to do.

Wonder why things are the way that they are in the place that you're visiting. Compare what you see to what you're used to seeing at home. Even if you're in a McDonalds, just like you would be at home, stop and ask: is that a new menu item? What kinds of people come here? Would there be this many bicycles outside the one back home? The idea here is to open up your mind and be challenged by the environment that you are in to promote growth. Learn and adapt from the new lessons that are available all around you.

- Slow down; give yourself room to focus.
- Connect to what's around you.
- Notice things.
- Let yourself be surprised.
- Look inward and reflect.

Intentional travel requires you to do things differently than you would on a typical vacation. Here, you are traveling for a purpose. That purpose can be anything that your heart desires. It may be something as grand as helping to build a school, or it may be as simple as spending twenty minutes a day talking with a local to develop a language. You're setting out with the goal of improving yourself or helping others—which in turn often enriches you as well.

Part of traveling intentionally should include time dedicated to the unknown. This last point is important: today, many of us have a tendency to plan every minute of an itinerary, leaving nothing to random chance. Part of traveling with a purpose is letting the purpose guide you more than a schedule; going down the rabbit hole may be better for your intent than the path you anticipated. As you interact with residents and other tourists you may receive a recommendation for a restaurant that is not on TripAdvisor, have a night out with a local you've made friends with, or stumble onto an idea for a daytrip somewhere that isn't in your travel guide. Be ready to deviate from the itinerary and leave time to go off-the-beaten-path.

As mentioned previously, how far you take intentional travel is entirely up to you but as it is with anything, you usually get out what you put in.

- Set one or two big goals, or lots of smaller goals, for your trip.
- Make choices that support those goals, both while planning and once you get there.
- Leave time and room for the unexpected.

Suggested Itinerary: Planning Your Trip

- If you're like most people, you probably want to—and have the means to—travel, at least a little. So get on it!
- If you have enough to live on, more money won't make you happy. Experiences will.
- Try experiential travel!

- Do activities that are unique to where you are visiting.
- Don't stay cooped up in a hotel or the tourist center.
- Connect with your location; interact with locals and other travelers to make the most out of your trip and build connections.

- Travel mindfully, i.e., with increased awareness.
- Travel intentionally, i.e., with certain goals in mind.
- Planning is great, but leave room for surprises.

.

PART 1

THE TRAVELER'S MIND

CREATIVITY

———

*"One travels to run away from routine, that dreadful routine
that kills all imagination and all our capacity for enthusiasm."*

—ELLA MAILLART

Roadmap

We've all heard the stories of famous writers who came
up with their most brilliant creations while traveling. J.K.
Rowling got the idea for Harry Potter while on a train ride
from Manchester back to London. Lin Manuel Miranda first
picked up a book about Alexander Hamilton at the airport
on the way to a beach vacation. And Ernest Hemingway's
trip to Spain served as the basis for *The Sun Also Rises.* (In
fact, as a world traveler, Hemingway drew almost all of his

inspiration from his adventures.) But you don't have to be trying to win the Pulitzer Prize or dying to write the next *Eat, Pray, Love* to be inspired by travel. Travel has the ability to make anyone more creative, regardless of their industry, or field—from academia and journalism to accounting and finance.

"In recent years, psychologists and neuroscientists have begun examining more closely what many people have already learned anecdotally: that spending time abroad may have the potential to affect mental change," writes Brent Crane in *The Atlantic*. "In general, creativity is related to neuroplasticity, or how the brain is wired. Neural pathways are influenced by environment and habit, meaning they're also sensitive to change: New sounds, smells, language, tastes, sensations, and sights spark different synapses in the brain and may have the potential to revitalize the mind."

This excerpt outlines the neuroscience behind something you probably already knew: we often need a break in the routine to revitalize us.

Personally, I don't know how many times I've heard "I need a vacation" from an overworked colleague or friend. And yes, a vacation will probably make them feel better. But you don't have to settle for a rest: you can develop your imagination at the same time.

In fact, psychologist Robert Epstein contends, "There's not really any evidence that one person is inherently more creative than another." His research shows that creativity is a skill that can be developed. Epstein says that to enhance creativity you should seek out challenges, broaden your knowledge, surround yourself with interesting things and people, and be sure to take note of your ideas. So, basically, take a trip and carry a travel diary. When he initiated an experiment that took these principles into account, the participants saw a 55% increase in their ability to come up with new ideas.

Travel is one of the most powerful tools we have to enhance our imagination and creativity. This is already common knowledge in most creative industries, so this chapter will instead focus on stories in the business and entrepreneurship space. This was done intentionally to demonstrate that the benefits of travel are not limited to artistic endeavors. It doesn't matter if you are working on a novel or if you are a business student, the right attitude while traveling can open up a whole new world of possibilities.

Top Sights

Argentine Innovation

"To move, to breathe, to fly, to float,
To gain all while you give,
To roam the roads of lands remote,
To travel is to live."

—HANS CHRISTIAN ANDERSEN, *THE FAIRY TALE*
OF MY LIFE (ALSO QUOTED IN A CHALLENGE
ON SEASON 19 OF *THE AMAZING RACE*)

Blake was an avid entrepreneur who worked very long hours to develop his business—some might call him a workaholic. As is common for many founders, Blake devoted a majority of his time to growing his business, leaving little time for personal enjoyment. But when he became a contestant on *The Amazing Race*, Blake had to resign himself to being different from his fellow entrepreneurs. Learning from his experience on the show, he became an avid traveler as well. He got in the habit of taking a month off each year in order to de-stress and enrich himself in a different part of the world.

"For me, the only way I could even have a thought of balance was this eleven months just going crazy, working as an entrepreneur, and then that month off," said Blake.

That month off would change his life.

In 2002, Blake and his sister Paige competed on the wildly popular second season of *The Amazing Race*. If you haven't seen the show, then I suggest you dust off your Hulu account and clear your schedule for the next month or two; the show has aired 30 seasons and counting. Over the course of a month, several teams travel around the world competing in mental and physical challenges for a cash prize of $1 million. While the prize is obviously the main motivation for competitors, most eliminated players say that the once-in-a-lifetime trip is a reward on its own.

It's my dream to be a contestant. And I'm pretty sure that after binge-watching 30 seasons, you'll feel the same way.

I won't spoil the season for you, so let's just say that Blake and Paige did quite well during their run. Argentina was among the many countries they visited on the show. In 2006, four years after his stint on the show, Blake decided to make his way back to Argentina.

Blake says he "always liked really immersing [him]self in whatever that country was known for." Since he wasn't much of a tango man, Blake decided to learn the national sport, polo, by enrolling in a training camp for his month off. At the same time, Blake dove head first into other parts of Argentine culture: he drank lots of Malbec (the national wine), learned some Spanish, and even started wearing a very popular local canvas shoe called the alpargata. The thought occurred to him that these shoes might have some commercial success if he were to bring them over to the United States. "But as with many half-formed ideas that came to me, I tabled it for the moment. My time in Argentina was supposed to be about fun, not work."

But the idea about the shoes came back to him again. "Toward the end of my trip, I met an American woman in a cafe who was volunteering on a shoe drive—a new concept to me. She explained that many kids lacked shoes, even in relatively well developed countries like Argentina, an absence that didn't just complicate every aspect of their lives—including essentials like attending school and getting water from the local well—but also exposed them to a wide range of diseases. Her organization collected shoes from donors and gave them to kids in need."

Though he'd never done anything like it, Blake wanted to help and experience this shoe drive first hand. He joined the next outing to collect shoes and then distribute them to the children.

The experience was incredible to him: "I spent a few days traveling from village to village with the woman and her group, and a few more traveling on my own, witnessing the intense pockets of poverty just outside the bustling capital. It dramatically heightened my awareness."

Afterward, Blake wanted to help even more. He started brainstorming how he could make a significant and lasting impact, even after leaving Argentina.

That's when it clicked: he had managed to encounter a problem and its solution all on this vacation. The alpargata shoes that he had been wearing were the answer. Sure, the shoes may have been successful in the U.S. on their own—but combined with the message of buying them for a good cause, they could really take off. So Blake called back home and took another month off—though this was no vacation, as he was intent on finding a manufacturer for his shoes. The rest is history.

Blake's story may have sounded familiar to you. The Blake that I've been talking about here is Blake Mycoskie, the Founder and Chief Shoe Giver of TOMS. At TOMS, for every pair of shoes purchased, a pair is given away to someone that is in need.

Yep, the founder of TOMS is named Blake—not Tom.

> **Facts & Figures: TOMS Shoes**
>
> Founded: 2006.
>
> Estimated Revenue: $400 million.
>
> Shoes Donated: Over 60 million.
>
> People Named Tom: A lot, probably, but not the founder.

Many people never knew that Blake got this idea thanks to his experiential trip to Argentina. Because he chose to immerse himself in the culture—all the way down to the shoes on his feet—Blake got a brilliant business idea he would never have thought of at home, regardless of his entrepreneurial acumen. And because he followed an unexpected interest in a local charity, he was able to turn that business idea into a philanthropic footwear fortune.

Souvenirs:

- Blake Mycoskie, entrepreneur and game show contestant, made a practice of taking one month off every year to immerse himself in a different culture.
  - Make a point of taking regular breaks from your life to try something new—the longer the trip, the better your opportunity to really dive deep into the unknown.

- Blake was inspired to start TOMS Shoes after he volunteered on a charity drive that collected shoes for Argentinians in need.
  - Sometimes, learning about new problems will set off the ol' mental light bulb better than staring at old ones. Going beyond tourism to get involved with local volunteer work lets you help yourself while serving the community you're visiting.
- If you have the chance, be a contestant on *The Amazing Race*.
  - And put in a good word for me! ;)

Thailand Gives You Wings

"Giving wings to people and ideas."

—RED BULL

Unfortunately, not all of us have the ability to take a month of continuous vacation to immerse ourselves in a culture and to let our internal gears start turning. However, that doesn't mean that a quick trip, even a working one, can't influence you to start something great.

For most of us, Dietrich Mateschitz is not a familiar name. This is by design. Although he's the richest man in Austria, Dietrich is fiercely private and rarely gives interviews. Nevertheless, you've probably heard of his company: Red Bull.

> **Facts & Figures: Red Bull**
>
> Founded: 1984.
>
> Estimated Revenue: €6.3 billion.
>
> Origin of the Drink: A Thai drink called KratingDaeng, which means "red gaur;" gaur is a type of bison, hence the name "Red Bull."

In 1982, Dietrich was working for Blendax, marketing toothpaste. While on a business trip to Asia, Dietrich discovered a popular Thai energy drink that helped him overcome his jet lag. Dietrich was so impressed with the results that he tracked down the creator of the drink, Chaleo Yoovidhya. He pitched a partnership that would bring the drink to Europe. Chaleo agreed, and even changed the ingredients to be more suited toward European tastes (i.e., less sweet).

Dietrich leveraged his prior experience working with Unilever and Blendax to handle marketing for his new company. The packaging was re-designed to the blue and silver can that we've all seen in the convenience store (Red Bull is now in over 170 countries), and the rest is history.

As an interesting note, the original Red Bull recipe is actually just a variation on a Japanese energy drink called Lipovitan D, which in turn was brought to Thailand and popularized by

Japanese expats in the 1960s. Chaleo recognized the drink's potential, so he altered the recipe slightly to suit Thai taste buds. Does this story sound familiar?

Rinse and repeat…

Souvenirs:

- On a business trip, Dietrich Mateschitz discovered an energy drink called Red Bull that cured his jet lag.
  - Regardless of the length of your trip, keep an eye out for what's new and different. Do they have something here that you can't bear to go back home without?
- Dietrich partnered with the drink's producer to bring the beverage to the European market and eventually world-wide.
  - Locals are the experts. You don't have to reinvent the wheel: you can make something great by learning from and working with those with experience.

Venti Italy to Go

"If the stewards of any consumer brand believe that they can create local relevance while sitting in a white tower somewhere in the U.S.—and dictating the ways in which consumers will react all over the world—they are on a collision course with time."

—HOWARD SCHULTZ

For many of us, we can't start our day without making a pilgrimage to the green and white logo of the holy siren. Starbucks is a global company—it's up there with Coca Cola for brands that you'll see regardless of where you step off the plane. But did you know that when the company first started in 1971, they sold only coffee beans? No prepared beverages except samples of the brewed beans.

Facts & Figures: Starbucks

Founded: 1971.

Estimated Revenue: $22.4 billion.

Origin of the Name: A character in Herman Melville's *Moby Dick*—thank goodness they didn't go with "Pequod."

Everything changed in the '80s, when the company's Director of Marketing, Howard Schultz, took a work trip to Milan. Howard noticed that the city was full of cafes that served espressos and other ready-made beverages. Even better, these cafes were more than just stores: they were gathering places for the locals, a real touchstone of the Italian culture.

"It was like an epiphany," Howard describes.

As soon as he got back to the U.S., Howard pleaded with the Starbucks head honchos to start selling beverages in-house and make Starbucks more of an experience rather than just a store. He even brought back recipes and videos of baristas making and serving coffee to demonstrate what he had witnessed. Starbucks execs agreed to a pilot, but despite its success, the owners did not want to pursue Howard's new model. But he would not be deterred. In 1985, Howard left Starbucks to see his vision through.

A year later, Howard opened his first Italian-style cafe in the U.S., called Il Giornale. It was an instant success. In fact, the cafe was so successful that just two years later, Howard bought Starbucks from the original owners. He combined the two companies under one name, and named himself the CEO.

Souvenirs:

- Howard Schultz, a Starbucks employee, was inspired to bring Italian cafe culture to the U.S. after a business trip to Milan.
  - Even if you think you're an expert in something, be open to the ways that other cultures treat it differently.
- Starbucks owners did not agree with Howard's vision, so he quit to start his own company.
  - Believe in your vision—especially when it has a proven track record of success elsewhere.

- Howard's iteration of a coffee company was so successful that he bought Starbucks two years later and became the CEO.
  - Not so much a learning point as a vengeance point. Good for you, Howard!

Getting Around

The stories in this chapter are just a few examples of a common pattern.

In 2004, Koel Thomae, an Aussie expat living in Colorado, had gone home to the Sunshine Coast to visit her family. On a walk to the beach she came across a vendor selling clear tubs of yogurt with fruit puree. She liked the recipe so much that she went back for more. When she returned to the States, Koel tried a hundred different varieties and brands to see if anything in the U.S. came close to what she had tasted on that beach. She didn't. Koel spent nearly three years working to bring that same recipe to the U.S. Her company, Noosa, had $170 million in sales in 2017.

The Sak, one of the largest handbag companies in the world, started when two childhood friends, Mark Talucci and Tod Elliott, left their corporate jobs to fulfill their dream of traveling the world. During a trip to Bali, they decided to start importing items that they found interesting back to the U.S. One item in particular, a rattan leather bag made out of an everyday Balinese sleeping mat, inspired them to narrow their focus to importing bags.

But let's be realistic. While many of us would love to start our own company, it's not for everyone. And there is nothing wrong with that. To start a new venture means giving up a steady paycheck and working tirelessly for the possibility of making it big. Many of us are risk-averse, or not in the place to take such risks—and there's nothing wrong with that. But there isn't just one type of person (like an entrepreneur or a founder) that could use more creativity and imagination.

Tyler Tervooren, founder of Riskology (a company that helps turn introverts into strong leaders) said, "By exposing yourself to new cultures and by putting yourself in new environments you can actually give your brain a new tool to use to solve a difficult problem." Moreover, you can apply these benefits to almost any field and position. Creativity is not just adapting ideas from other cultures and making it your own. New environments provide additional inputs to your brain to stimulate problem-solving that you can apply to any aspect of your life. So, travel can help you come up with a brand new way of converting sunlight to energy, inspire you to want to pursue architecture as a career, or tip the scale as to whether you want to cook Italian instead of Mexican for dinner tonight.

Adam Galinsky, a social psychologist and professor at Columbia Business School, has conducted extensive research relating to the effects of travel on the human psyche. (We'll be talking about his work a lot in this book.) In one study, Professor Galinsky and his team gathered industry data of creative directors from 270 high-end fashion houses over an eleven-year period (2000-2010). The research conclusively showed that fashion directors who had lived abroad more consistently released creative fashion lines compared to those who had not. (For those of you wondering how the study measured the creativity of a fashion line, it was based on ratings from trade journalists, fashion critics, and buyers.) Furthermore, the longer a designer had lived abroad, the more creative their fashion output. In fact, the research team concluded that depth, the number of years worked abroad in their professional career, "is the most critical dimension for achieving creative innovations."

The study concluded, "Foreign experiences, especially ones with significant duration and spread across a number of culturally diverse countries, may provide career boosts to individuals and help enhance the creativity of the organizations they join. The first step toward being the next Karl Lagerfeld might start with something as simple as finding an opportunity to work abroad."

Again, this finding is not unique to any one industry. In another study co-authored by Adam Galinsky, research showed that "the longer undergraduate and MBA students had lived abroad, the more creative they were on standard psychological tests of creativity."

The point is, anyone can benefit from travel. You don't have to be a young prodigy to get inspired. In fact, it took Dietrich a decade to finish his business degree—and he was nearly 40 when he discovered the drink that would become Red Bull. It doesn't matter where you come from or where you go: you simply need to be mindful when you travel. Keep your eyes open and your brain active and there is an endless world of possibilities out there. You don't need to invent, write, or do something that is completely new and unheard of. As we've learned from these stories, slight modifications—or even no modifications—are all that is often needed to introduce something groundbreaking.

Per Professor Galinsky, "The key, critical process is multicultural engagement, immersion, and adaptation. Someone who lives abroad and doesn't engage with the local culture will likely get less of a creative boost than someone who travels abroad and really engages in the local environment."

Once you get that creative boost, harness it with your own knowledge and skills. The people that we read about in this chapter paid attention to their surroundings and then recognized an opportunity. Their experiences were no different from thousands if not millions of other travelers before them. But those other people were not as mindful, or failed to connect their experiences abroad with opportunities back home.

Blake had no experience in the shoe industry, but he did know entrepreneurship. So he used his knowledge of starting businesses to grow this new one. Dietrich had never worked in the beverage space but he had an extensive career in marketing. His tactics—guerrilla marketing, athletic sponsorships, and targeting young partygoers—are why Red Bull stands at the top of its industry. Prior to starting his company, Howard had years of experience in the coffee industry, so he immediately recognized a good concept when he saw it—so much so that he believed in his own vision even when his bosses didn't.

Again, this doesn't have to be about multi-million dollar ideas. Simply taking yourself out of your normal routine— and the farther outside your comfort zone and the more different the environment, the better—can be a catalyst for creativity. Travel enriches us with experiences that can be used as tools to apply to all aspects of our lives. While it is up to each individual how they choose to use these tools, it is still a solid bet that the more tools you have at your disposal, the more opportunities will open up for you.

Suggested Itinerary: Sparking Your Creativity

- Got a problem you can't solve? Waiting for the inspiration that never seems to strike? Sometimes, your imagination just needs a change of scenery to get that kick start.
- When traveling, be vigilant for anything that is new to you. Ask:
  - Will this work where I am from?
  - Can I make small modifications to fit local preferences?
  - Why hasn't this been introduced to my market yet?
  - Can I leverage my skills or resources to do a better job with the idea, product, or service I see?
- If you have the ability, go for an extended trip. The deeper your exposure, the higher your chance for enlightenment.

PERSPECTIVE

———

"The real voyage of discovery consists not in seeking new landscapes, but in having new eyes."

—MARCEL PROUST, *IN SEARCH OF LOST TIME*

Roadmap

The internet, television, and social media have done a wonderful job of making the world seem smaller than ever. After all, we are always just one click away from pretty much anything that our hearts desire. A computer screen can show you the streets of any city, and pictures of some of the most remote places in the world are at your fingertips. But is this entirely a good thing?

Some argue that there are downsides to the meteoric increase in the information available to us. Rather than make our world larger, the world has shrunk. And when we think of the world as small, it's easier to think of ourselves as the center of the universe, and our problems grow bigger to match. But if we could see ourselves as we are, as tiny specks in a great wide world, then the insurmountable mountains of our problems begin to look like frail sandcastles.

If someone were to ask you, "Is $10,000 a good return on an investment?" you might be tempted to say, "Yes, ten grand sounds pretty good to me!" But what if you were then told that this return was based on an investment of $10 million? Suddenly, that $10,000 seems like a terrible return. You could have made more than ten times that amount by just sticking your money in a savings account.

It's impossible to decide what is "good" without the proper frame of reference. Context is the only way to make sense of a life and its problems. By seeing the world, we are able to see how others live their lives in comparison to ours. Maybe you are not as poor as you thought yourself to be. Maybe you are more intelligent than you give yourself credit for. And just maybe there are even weirder people out there than your family that embarrasses you at every turn!

The people in this chapter come from different backgrounds and are in very different stages of their lives. This is intentional. It does not matter if you are a student, climbing the corporate ladder toward becoming a CEO, or breaking into the party industry—travel can help you put your life in perspective and guide you toward what you really want out of life.

Top Sights

Liberia & Self-Liberation

"Spending time in a leper colony and many remote villages, I put a face to the world's 1.2 billion living in poverty. Those living on less than $365 a year—money I used to blow on a bottle of Grey Goose vodka at a fancy club."

—SCOTT HARRISON

It's New Year's Eve at a mansion party full of beautiful people in Punta Del Este, a resort city on the coast of Uruguay. The wait staff is keeping the high-end alcohol flowing, and there's no shortage of food courtesy of professional cooks. Scott Harrison should be having one of the best times of his life.

He's not. In fact, he wants nothing but to get away from the booze, drugs, and other vices that surround him.

Scott had been making a ton of money as a club promoter in New York City for a decade. He was so successful that at one point he and his associate were getting paid $4,000 a month by Bacardi and Budweiser—each—just to drink their brands in public. He had an incredible apartment in the city, drove a fancy BMW, wore an expensive Rolex, and dated a woman that was on the cover of *Elle* magazine. At 28, he already had almost everything a person could want. But he wasn't happy.

"I realized that I was spiritually bankrupt, I was emotionally bankrupt, I was certainly morally bankrupt. It was this endless pursuit of more. And I was surrounded by much wealthier and [more] successful people and I realized that they weren't all happy either and there would just never be enough. It was almost like the game of musical chairs where the music stopped and I looked around and there was nowhere to sit. I just felt unsettled."

At that party in Uruguay, Scott had an epiphany. He decided he needed to get out of the nightclub business and go cold turkey on his vices. He wanted to do something beyond partying and getting wasted. He asked himself, "What would the opposite of my life look like? Well, if I'm this selfish, hedonistic, drug-addled nightclub promoter who's done nothing for the poor, nothing for anyone else, what would it look like to actually help people in need?"

So Scott decided that he would dedicate the next year of his life to helping the poor. He applied to every charitable organization that he could think of.

He was denied by all but one.

Mercy Ships agreed to let him "volunteer" for them as a photojournalist in Liberia—if Scott paid them $500 a month for the privilege. He did just that.

Facts & Figures: Mercy Ships

Founded: 1978.

Mission: To provide humanitarian aid primarily through free healthcare services to port cities around the world.

Ships In Use: Although they've had as many as three ships in operation in the past, Mercy currently has only one ship—though it is the largest non-governmental hospital ship in the world.

For the next two years, Scott documented life-altering surgeries aboard Mercy Ships. He was inspired to see doctors remove tumors and fix cleft palates, but he was also exposed to general human suffering unlike anything he had witnessed before.

"There was this powerful moment for me where on our screening day—so this was my third day in Africa—the government had given us a football stadium, a soccer stadium, to triage the patients as they would come in and I knew that we had 1,500 surgery slots. I remember jumping into a Land Rover at five in the morning, I had scrubs on, I had my two Nikon cameras around my neck and I'm like, 'Are 1,500 sick people really going to turn up?'"

As it turned out, 5,000 people showed up.

"So there was this moment for me of, 'Oh my gosh, we're going to send 3,000 people home who have come with hope.'"

It didn't help that Liberia had recently gone through a civil war.

"Bullet holes are everywhere. You just couldn't take a picture without capturing bullet holes."

But it wasn't the images of war that left the deepest impact. Even a privileged kid like Scott knew war was terrible. What shocked him so much about the poverty and pain was learning that the bulk of the issues that these people faced stemmed from the lack of clean water.

"You're in disbelief because it looks like a brown, viscous swamp. It's not even chocolate milk, it's like thick chocolate milk. I would watch these children bathing in dirty water, drinking dirty water, washing their clothes in dirty water, and I learned that 50% of the country was drinking bad water. Again, I was taking pictures of this, I'm back on the ship and I'm sharing what I'm seeing with the doctors and surgeons and they're like, 'Yeah, duh, of course. We know so much of the sickness is related to water.'"

He discovered that nearly one in ten people in the world did not have access to clean water. This number was staggering for him. "Dirty water is responsible for more death in the world than all forms of violence, including war."

But the problem didn't just end there. Many of these people—and especially women and young girls—spent hours every day going to fetch this filthy water, often at the cost of going to school.

Scott ended up staying on in Liberia for two years, rather than the one he had planned. When he finally returned to New York in 2006, he was determined to do something about the global water problem. But all he knew how to do was to throw parties... so that is exactly what he did.

To celebrate his 31st birthday, Scott had a club donate their space for a party. He then charged each entrant $20, all of which was donated to repair water wells in a refugee camp in northern Uganda. He raised $15,000 that night.

"The skill that I really learned was storytelling and promoting, and I was promoting the idea that if you get past the velvet rope and spend all of your money buying expensive champagne and being with beautiful people then your life has meaning." Instead, he started to promote the belief that "If you're working to end needless suffering around the world, then your life has meaning and purpose."

Scott then used some of his hard-earned journalism skills to document the process of where and how the money was used. Each person that had donated received details about where their donation went, including photos. Those partygoers turned out to love that feature. "People would not believe that a charity would bother to report to them on a $20 gift and that something happened to the money that they could see, that they could connect with."

Seeing the reaction to his party, Scott knew he was on to something. "As I'm talking about setting up a charity I realized that so many of my friends don't trust charities. In fact, I learned that 42% of people in America alone don't trust charities. … They said, 'Oh, I don't give to charities, charities are black holes. I don't know where my money would go. I don't know how much of it would actually reach the people. Charities are ineffective, they're bureaucratic, the CEO is probably just trying to make millions of dollars for himself and driving a Mercedes Benz around.'"

Scott came up with a new model for his charity. He decided 100% of donations would go entirely toward the cause, with absolute transparency on of all the charity's finances. He funded operations for the charity separately, with a distinct bank account funded through other individual donors.

This is how Charity: Water was born. Since then, the charity has been consistently praised as one of the most innovative of its kind, especially for its transparency. To date, Scott's organization has donated more than a quarter of a billion dollars toward funding 30,000 water projects that helped over eight million people in need.

Souvenirs:

- Scott Harrison left behind a lucrative career as a nightclub promoter to search for deeper meaning and to try to help others.
  - As we've discussed before, money doesn't buy happiness. But perspective can make all the difference.

- Scott's two-year stint as a photojournalist in Liberia showed him that what he really wanted to do was make the world a better place through providing clean water.
  - Although there are many problems in the world, a mindful traveler can turn a problem into a calling.
- Scott used the skills from his prior life—club promotion—to begin working toward his philanthropic dreams.
  - All the negativity associated with a previous career can be turned around for the positive if put in a new context, such as working toward a goal you believe in.

Move Out, Stand Out

"It is hard to stand out if you do exactly what everyone else does, and going to New York for finance or consulting is exactly what everyone else does."

—NICK ERARDI

Nick Erardi is not the type of person you would expect to find among the graduate school crowd at Georgetown University. He's a former minor-league baseball player, standing at an intimidating 6 foot 5 inches, with a muscular build and fiery red hair. But, as is often the case, looks have a way of being deceiving: Nick is one of the most approachable and big-hearted people that I've had the opportunity to know.

After graduation, Nick stuck around D.C. and started working two part-time jobs—an entrepreneurial venture and some temporary consulting work—while looking for a full-time opportunity that would make him feel fulfilled and afford him the lavish lifestyle of his dreams. But after three years of instability and temporary projects, Nick was losing steam. But everything changed thanks to an impromptu trip to Calgary and Thailand.

Nick had always wanted to visit Thailand. Finding a lull in his part-time projects, Nick decided to pursue his dream of going to the other side of the world and training in Muay Thai. (Muay Thai is Thailand's national sport. It's like kick-boxing, but better.)

And Thailand delivered. "The people there were so kind and happy that I felt at home, even though I was as far away from home as humanly possible." Nick's biggest take-away from that month-long trip had nothing to do with his martial arts training; instead, he learned that it doesn't matter where you are, "as long as the people are welcoming you can make any place your home." Traveling to the other side of the world changed his perspective on everything; he learned that new environments were not as scary as he feared. In fact, new places can be more inviting than your own home.

For the first time in a long time, Nick was fired up about his life path. He realized he was stuck in a rut in D.C., and it was high time he pursued his options elsewhere. That elsewhere revealed itself on the next stop after Thailand.

Nick visited a longtime friend in Calgary, Canada, a.k.a. a slightly less dreamy locale. But Nick shared his insights from Thailand with his friend, and as the two of them were having a great time in Calgary, the friend suggested that Nick move there.

It felt like a risk, but then again, Nick's newly broadened perspective made him think it wasn't so risky: there was no language barrier to worry about, he enjoyed the city, and the friend offered him a part-time job at his business while Nick explored his options. So Nick went back to D.C. and began packing his bags. He realized that if he could have such an amazing experience abroad in a country with a completely different culture and language, moving to Canada was only going to be a minor inconvenience—with a potentially huge payoff.

In Canada—even more so than in business school—Nick stood out. "You stand out if you put yourself in Calgary where most candidates went to University of Calgary and are Canadian; when they see you have a great pedigree that is different, [but you're] living locally, you usually get a call back. You put yourself on a different path by locating yourself in a place that doesn't immediately make sense." His change of scenery worked. Shortly after relocating, Nick was hired as a full-time consultant at Accenture, a Fortune 500 global management consulting and professional services firm. Nick probably could not have gotten a job at Accenture's New York or D.C. offices, where he would have the same background as every other candidate, but Calgary welcomed him with open arms.

More likely than not, each of us is not as unique as we like to think that we are. Even if you graduated at the top of your class, there are 2,617 other accredited college institutions in the U.S.—all of which had someone new at the top, every year. In Florida, you walk by a million seashells without a second look; but if you saw one in Kabul, you would pause and maybe even pick it up. Again, it's a question of perspective. When is a big move not so scary? Where will you stand out from the crowd? If Nick had stayed in D.C., he probably would have spent a lot more time looking for a good job, or he would have settled for a less prestigious position.

But maybe you think Nick's situation was just dumb luck—he ended up in the right place at the right time. Well, what makes Nick's example even more credible is that he is not unique, not even in his own office. One of his coworkers at Accenture has a similar success story: an American who graduated from Cornell, he ended up finding a much better job in Calgary than he could have gotten in the States. Even better, both Nick and this colleague have continued to reap the benefits of standing out. Nick reports that the two of them are often put on top client projects for the simple reason that they went to universities with better known brand names than their Canadian counterparts.

Being different does not guarantee success. Of course, you need a lot of good qualities to excel, but in these competitive times, you should take every edge you can. But if you get perspective on yourself, you can make smarter choices that lead to better outcomes.

Souvenirs:

- Nick's trip to Thailand made him realize that he was in a rut back in D.C.; he needed a change of location to get a fresh start.
  - Sometimes we don't see the writing on the wall unless we step back and reevaluate.
  - The more you travel, the more you recognize that the world is not so scary; even the most foreign places can be welcoming.
- By moving to Calgary, Nick forced employers to look at him from a different perspective. In D.C., he was just like everyone else; but in Canada, he stood out and leveraged himself into a job that he really wanted.

- Perspective goes both ways: the way the world appears to you and the way you appear to the world. If you're not happy with the way you fit in (or fail to fit in), make the world look at you differently.

The Comeback Kid

"The more I traveled the more comfortable I became with myself. It gave me the breathing room I needed to think about what I wanted to pursue as my next path."

—ARI GORDON

Ari Gordon is very ambitious for his age. In his four years at the University of Washington, Ari started or was involved with four separate startups. He remains involved in two of these: a recipe app called SagePlate, and another company centered on Kombucha.

Ari's accomplishments in college owe everything to the detour he took before he got there. Ari took a gap year after high school, funded by a few months' work waiting tables and running a landscaping company. Eventually, he saved up enough to go on a five-month backpacking adventure across South America followed by a three-month stay in Israel with distant family in a kibbutz. These travels gave him the motivation and relentless drive that propelled him to entrepreneurship despite his youth.

"Traveling in South America opened up my eyes to so much about the world, I felt inspired to want to be like many of the talented people that I met. While in Israel, I learned how people can live such different lives than the U.S., but at the same time we have so many similarities to each other. The experience as a whole made me much more social; it made me more open to all walks of life."

Over the course of his travels in South America and Israel, he interacted with a wide assortment of people—everyone from professional musicians to athletes, from drug lords to engineers. Ari wanted to model himself after the people that inspired him most on his travels, and that led him to entrepreneurship.

For the first two years of college, Ari was very active in getting his businesses off the ground. But eventually he got burnt out from trying to do so much while keeping up with class work. "I was anxious. I was trying to do too many things at school; I wasn't able to focus on what my task at hand was."

His solution was more travel: he took a break from school to visit Thailand and Bhutan. This time, he wasn't looking outward for inspiration. Instead, he focused inwards, falling in love with the practice of meditation. Although he had previously been introduced to meditation, he honed the skill by joining a monastery in Thailand. He says of this time, "It helped immensely. I look back at before, during, and after and there is a significant difference with how I live my life."

He returned to school with renewed vigor, and continued to work on his two businesses through graduation. Ari took graduation as a time to reassess: his businesses were not performing as well as he expected, but he didn't know what he was doing wrong. Rather than continue to struggle, he stepped back from those projects and chose to build his skill set. He lived for a year in Barcelona, where he worked in the marketing department of a travel agency. "The experience came with more loneliness and time to myself but that was awesome in its own way since it gave me the time again to think about what I am trying to do and where I am trying to go in life." Afterward, he returned to his two companies, and both are now nearly ready to launch.

As you may have noticed, there is a pattern to the journey that Ari took to get his ideas from design to fruition: he works extremely hard, to the point of exhaustion; then, he refreshes his perspective by stepping back from his work and going abroad; and then he repeats the cycle anew. Many entrepreneurs follow a similar regimen—as do people in all walks of life. But Ari doesn't just take vacations—he takes each trip as an opportunity to learn something new, so that each time he comes back to his work, he is a better version of himself.

Souvenirs:

- Before college, Ari Gordon took a gap year to travel in South America and Israel.
  - If you have the chance to take time off to travel before starting school or a job, take it! (More on this later.)
- Even after he started working, Ari used extended trips away as opportunities to refocus his priorities and learn new things.
  - Taking a step away from your normal environment—even if it's into another working environment—can relieve stress and reinvigorate you.
  - And the next-level traveler doesn't just take the time to relax: you can pick up skills that will help you find new ways to tackle your problems.

Getting Around

At the start of *The Traveler's Edge*, I mentioned that I would present stories from some of the most successful people that I know and know of. What I didn't do was define what "success" means. My version of success may be completely different from yours.

For example, if you define success as how much money you make, then Scott became less successful after traveling, because he makes less money at the helm of Charity: Water than when he did as a club promoter. But if you define success by how much of an impact someone makes on the less fortunate, or by how fulfilled an individual is with their life, then Scott is much more successful now. It's all about our perception.

I don't think of anyone in this book as categorically more successful than anyone else. Scott, Nick, and Ari are all happy with what they are doing with their lives. Scott may be reaching more people with his work, but he also started out with a rolodex full of wealthy and influential people. Besides, Scott explicitly sought out work that would help as many people as possible, whereas Nick and Ari had different goals. Ari is passionate about his entrepreneurship, and Nick wanted to stand out in a crowded field.

In his book *Free Will*, Sam Harris argues that the subject of his book doesn't exist. He contends, based on scientific data, that your brain has already decided what you are going to do before you are consciously aware of it. Our experiences in life program our brains with how to react and what choices to make. Sam says we are, very literally, the sum of our experiences.

By this logic, if you train your brain with events where you act independently, you will make similar choices in the future. If you meet people from many different cultures and are exposed to different ways of doings things, you are more likely to react well when new and unexpected things come your way. The first time you drive a car can be scary;

but if you've done it many times, in different places and in all kinds of weather, you'll be a more confident and capable driver. In the same way, more travel will make you a more open-minded and level-headed person. While some would argue that genetics also contributes to this equation, most people would agree that accumulating experiences helps us grow and gain perspective. And the best way to accumulate these experiences is to step out of you current sphere and go out into the wide world.

Furthermore, these experiences go beyond just making you a more competent person: they allow you to have a better understanding of yourself. In another research paper published in *Organizational Behavior and Human Decision Processes*, Professor Galinsky examined how living abroad can lead to a clearer concept of self: "Our results indicate that living abroad leads to a clearer sense of self because it prompts self-discerning reflections on whether parts of their identity truly define who they are or merely reflect their cultural upbringing. Furthermore, it is the depth (the length of time lived abroad) rather than the breadth (the number of foreign countries lived in) of living abroad experiences that enhances self-concept clarity."

So, as promised, the more context you get—measured in length of time immersing yourself in another culture—the better you understand yourself. "Finally, our results highlight an important consequence of the link between living abroad and self-concept clarity: career decision-making clarity. Our research suggests that going far from home can lead one closer to the self, with implications for significant life decisions."

Thus by gaining this clarity about ourselves, we are able to make clearer decisions about everything else in our lives, including those choices we make in our careers. So if you are struggling with hard decisions or just generally feel out of balance, maybe it's time for another trip.

Suggested Itinerary: Expanding Your Perspective

- Regardless of where you are in life, an extended trip can give you clarity and space to reflect on yourself.
    - Transitional times, like before starting school or a new job, are often a great opportunity to take a few weeks, months, or even a year away.
    - Pro tip for new jobs: negotiate a few weeks off prior to starting. If they are not flexible, ask your current employer if they really need you for the full two-week notice period. These periods are often for show—you can even offer to work remotely while you explore the world. Besides, what are they going to do... fire you?
- If you're following the same path everyone else is, but it's not working for you, consider changing course. If you feel yourself

falling to the middle of the pack, find a place where you can stand out.

- Part of perspective is figuring out where the best place for you is, and getting yourself there.

- Stepping away from your everyday world lets you assess what skills you have, and what you need to develop.

  - Distance can give you the perspective you need to decide what parts of your life you want to embrace and what you want to move away from; what you can take with you, and what you need to find.

CONFIDENCE

———

"Man often becomes what he believes himself to be. If I keep on saying to myself that I cannot do a certain thing, it is possible that I may end by really becoming incapable of doing it. On the contrary, if I have the belief that I can do it, I shall surely acquire the capacity to do it even if I may not have it at the beginning."

—MAHATMA GANDHI

Roadmap

We've all heard that believing in yourself is one of the most critical ingredients for success. Science agrees. Although there are many definitions of success, let's take for example the idea that success is reflected in how much money you make. According to research conducted by Professors Demarree, Petty, and Briñol based on a survey of over 150,000 Americans, the higher your confidence level, the higher your income.

But how do you build that self-assurance that will propel you to even greater heights? This chapter will focus on how you can increase your confidence through successful experiences while traveling. We will also take a deeper look at how having confidence allows you to take control of, and change, your life.

Confidence comes in many forms—it isn't simply an all-encompassing belief in yourself. No one is good at everything, but not being good at something, especially just because of a lack of experience, shouldn't keep you from doing it. Confidence is a skill that can be learned through experience and repetition. It won't make you good at everything, but it will make you more comfortable with your ability to do challenging things. With time, things that once seemed foreign can become commonplace.

If you are already a top performer at school or in your company, then you probably don't need the confidence boost—keep doing what you're doing, or take a break and get a well-earned drink, rock star! But if you're stressed about getting the job that you desperately want, or you're worried you should be doing better in work or school, this chapter is here to help. Often, stepping away from the environment that is pressuring you is the best thing that you can do for yourself. Instead, put yourself in a different place, where you can take risks and give yourself room to fail or succeed—without that debilitating fear of the consequences.

Hard work does pay off. One of my favorite sayings reminds me that "everything yields to diligence." But I also believe the old adage that "one definition of insanity is doing the exact same thing over and over again, expecting different results." That. Is.Bananas. So let's try something else, and see what we learn.

Top Sights

Pre-Meds without Borders

"Travel is a catalyst for growth because you are either going to learn something about other people or you are going to learn something about yourself."

—MICHAEL SOBALVARRO

When most people think of travel, they think of two distinct categories: business or pleasure. But there is a third kind, often overlooked: volunteer travel, or voluntourism. Voluntourism is when volunteers contribute their time to work for organizations or causes outside their home countries. The most common example of this is alternative spring break, where students forego a week of partying in the Bahamas to build houses in communities in need. But voluntourism can also be an opportunity jump-start a new career by taking advantage of work experience that may not be as easily accessible at home.

Michael Sobalvarro is a Translation Science Research Intern at Georgetown University. (Michael's work is not the translation you may be thinking of—think biology, not linguistics.) While he has always been an outstanding student (he got a full scholarship to Georgetown's pre-med program), he credits a lot of his personal growth to a week-long volunteer trip to Honduras.

As a freshman, Michael saw that some of his classmates were starting their own businesses, and others were gaining real-world skills through internship programs. He noticed that there was no similar opportunity to build clinical skills available to those in the pre-med program. There's good reason for this lack of on-the-job training for undergraduates. In the U.S., pre-med students like Michael are not typically allowed to interact with patients because they don't have the necessary experience and knowledge.

However, some parts of the world are so lacking in trained medical staff that novices like Michael are better than the alternative; thus, students are permitted to work with real patients under the supervision of real doctors. Michael discovered an organization called Global Brigades, which facilitates this trade-off: the local population gets free medical help, while the volunteers get firsthand experience that is incredibly hard to come by domestically.

Facts & Figures: Global Brigades

Founded: 2007.

Volunteers: Over 65,000 from over 8,000 universities and clubs.

People Helped: Over 1 million in four countries.

Vision: To improve equality (yes, you read that right) of life by igniting the largest student-led social responsibility movement on the planet.

So Michael organized a group of his fellow pre-med students to help raise money to fund the trip to El Paraiso, Honduras, where they could help provide much-needed medical attention to the local population.

Unfortunately, Honduras was in a state of turmoil. Michael and his peers were working just outside the capital,

Tegucigalpa, which Spanish journalist Alberto Arce once described as "the most dangerous capital city in the world without a declared war." The country was in dire need of medical help: "In 2012 and 2013, more people were murdered in Honduras than in Iraq, even though the population in Honduras is three times smaller." Nevertheless, where others saw danger and despair, Michael saw an opportunity to help his fellow man, and grow into his profession at the same time.

"It was weird being put into a position that I wasn't in before. I had never been a health provider." But Michael found the courage to take on this new role in part because he saw how different his life in Honduras was from his life back home in D.C. In the U.S., he was no doctor; but in Honduras, he had to think and act like one. As he described, "Travel gives you a different identity. ... I wasn't a real doctor but I was helping diagnose people in a hospital setting. It caused me to view myself differently. ... I went from being an 18-year-old who would normally need to look around for help from an adult, to being the adult in this situation."

In these stressful circumstances, Michael found that "the safety net is removed and it forces you to confront things about yourself that are both positive and negative." He and his fellow volunteers quickly learned their strengths and weaknesses. They were all faced with the option of adapting or buckling under the pressure. In response, they learned. They didn't just learn how to be doctors: they learned how to deal with overwhelming, high-pressure, and unexpected situations.

Michael would never have been able to handle the work on his own. People came from miles around for medical help, and teamwork was vital to the everyday operations of the medical center. In a setting with so much at stake, Michael and his peers learned their own skills, but they also learned to trust each other. Between their newfound abilities and the faith of their coworkers and patients, Michael and the other students saw their confidence in themselves surge.

The trip provided such tremendous value to him, his fellow classmates, and the community in Honduras that Michael later arranged two more.

Souvenirs:

- Voluntourism provides great opportunities for individuals to develop skills or have experiences that are not available to them domestically.
- Michael's college did not offer a program for pre-med students to develop real doctor skills, so he found and partnered with an organization on his own.

- Just because something is not available at your school, in your city, or for your job doesn't mean that it can't be done. Be innovative and create your own opportunity.
- Michael and his classmates did a week of clinical work under doctors' supervision in Honduras, gaining experience years ahead of their peers.
  - Doing a trial run earlier in your career can minimize your learning curve in the future and put you ahead of your peers.
  - Use your opportunity abroad to gain confidence to take back home with you.

Waffles Topped with Enlightenment

"I am not scared of anything anymore because I know I'll be able to figure it out. That fear is just gone."

—JESSICA ROHRER

Jessica Rohrer grew up in Northern Virginia, went to college at James Madison University, and spent her career working in D.C., providing specialized lending in the banking industry. For most of her life, Jessica had never lived anywhere but her home state and the D.C. area. But in 2016, her husband was given the opportunity to work in Belgium. So she decided to pack up her bags and move to Europe—with no job in sight.

"Before I decided to quit and go to Europe for an extended period of time, I was doing really well. I was making a lot of money; I was on the fast track to management. I take the metro into work every single day and I remember I was standing on the escalator on the way to the office and it was silent, everyone was staring at their phone and I remember looking around and thinking to myself, 'Is this what I want for the rest of my life, is this what I want it to be like?' No, even though it is really scary, I'm going to Europe."

The plan was that Jessica would rely on her husband's income until she could find a job in Belgium. They would enjoy their time abroad, including time to travel across Europe together, and afterward would return to the U.S. and settle down. However, shortly after the couple moved to Belgium, they separated. Jessica was faced with a very tough decision: go back to the comforts of home, or stay the course and see her plan through—alone. She chose the latter.

Jessica had never traveled alone before, and she was surprised by how challenging it was. "Traveling as a solo female proved to be a difficult test; I had to learn to trust myself again. I had no one to depend on. Belgium was on high alert from a terror attack, which did not help the situation. It is very easy to get caught up in all the bad things that you hear are happening in the world, but going out there and seeing all the beauty and wonder helps to alleviate that negativity.

And it is completely worth it. I learned so much about new people and other cultures; my horizons were constantly being broadened."

Finding a job abroad was yet another challenge. Although English is widely spoken in Belgium, most financial institutions there require employees to be proficient in French and Dutch. Like most Americans, Jessica did not have those extra languages under her belt. Rather than be discouraged when she couldn't get a job similar to her old one, Jessica decided to start her own business. Her solo travels had given her confidence in her ability to work through whatever life threw at her.

Her travels also taught her something else: there were a lot of expats who needed financial advice, for everything from investments to saving for retirement. Jessica had the financial background to help, and she signed up for two more courses to build her acumen: a business development course to learn how to promote herself, and French classes to better integrate and to help expand her reach in her new home. She even studied for and earned a Series 65 license, which allowed her to provide additional investment advice.

"I formed a different perspective on life while traveling; I got a glimpse at what really matters. I was stressed out before going abroad. I was working at a big bank in D.C., waking up unhappy, and I was worrying about all these things that just don't seem important anymore. Traveling gave me a broader perspective on life, on what is important and what really matters, and what life is like for other people; how it's different and how it's the same. Everyone is just looking to find happiness when it comes down to it."

Jessica left everything she knew behind, and still managed to build a great life in Belgium. And from the vantage point of this new Jessica, she had time to reflect on what she wanted the rest of her life to look like, and the confidence to bring that vision to fruition.

From a very early age, our lives are structured. We're supposed to go to school, then college, then work, climb the corporate ladder, have children, and finally retire. If you make it through all that, feel free to do whatever your 75-year-old heart desires. Self-reflection doesn't have a clear spot on this path. "Being at home, sometimes you find yourself on autopilot and before you know it five years have passed. When I went abroad, it gave me the opportunity to see where I wanted to go next in my life."

Jessica ended up returning to the U.S., though she moved to Nashville rather than go back to D.C. She says, "It's hard to explain just how different my life is. My life now looks nothing like my life before I left for Belgium. It's crazy. I realized

I wanted to make an impact on people's lives and I didn't feel as though I was doing that before. I found a job that I actually like (which is possible!). Now I'm working at a non-profit lender helping to develop the small-business community in Nashville."

A lot of you reading this book can likely sympathize with Jessica's situation. The majority of us live to work rather than work to live, and this is why so many of us face an existential crisis at some point in our lives. Because she traveled Europe on her own, Jessica found a way of life that actually made her happy. "I had a different lifestyle in Europe, one where people actually take coffee breaks, lunch breaks and vacations, even long vacations. When I came back to the U.S., I knew I couldn't go back to my old life. I wanted to create a lifestyle working in a job I was passionate about and where life was about more than just work."

And now she does.

Souvenirs:

- Jessica had never taken the opportunity to reflect on her life choices. Although she was doing well in her job, she was not happy.
  - It's hard to really reflect on something as big as your life path while you're staying on it. Even if you do not take

a trip to the other side of the world, take some time off and away to figure out what you really want.

- Jessica was in a tough position after moving to Belgium because she split from her husband. She made the best of her situation and came out stronger and happier as a result.
  - Life often throws curve balls when we least expect them. Sometimes, the answer to tumult isn't to look for a new anchor, but to take the opportunity to embrace the unknown.
  - If you're brave enough, solo travel can be the most rewarding and life-changing way to go.
- Jessica's time abroad gave her the confidence and inspiration to change both her job and her philosophy about working.
  - You do not need to travel across Europe to see what is and isn't working in your life, but you do need to do things that take you out of your element and show you how strong you can be.
- Even when she returned to the U.S., Jessica changed her lifestyle to reflect the values that she had learned were important to her.
  - Whatever you learn when you're away, you can find a way to incorporate it into your old life—or use it to forge a new one.

Ivy League (Un)Bound

"When it comes to confidence and motivation and self-efficacy, the things that really matter when it comes to making your

way in the world, relative position matters more than absolute position."

— MALCOLM GLADWELL

"Pressure can burst a pipe, or pressure can make a diamond." The quote highlights the diamond, but most people end up being the pipe. Nick's story about changing your location to change your perspective brings up a good question: is it really good for us to all be clamoring for the same top schools, top cities, and top jobs?

Like everything, it depends. What kind of person are you? Do you thrive in a competitive environment? Can you find a way to stand out among the best? Let's see what author, journalist, public speaker, and Canadian extraordinaire Malcolm Gladwell has to say.

In 2013, Malcolm gave a thought-provoking speech for Zeitgeist (Google's version of a TED Talk) on the effect our environment has on our ability and success. He said, "As human beings, we do not form our self-assessments based on our standing in the world. We form our self-assessments based on our standing … in our immediate circle, on those in the same boat as ourselves." That means that regardless of how intelligent, successful, and talented we are, we will feel inadequate in certain social circles.

Let's consider an example. Brian Chesky is the CEO and co-founder of Airbnb, and by all rights his biography is impressive enough to make any of us green with envy. His company is valued at over $30 billion and is known worldwide, he personally is a billionaire, and he isn't even 40 yet. But what if we were to put him in a room with Elon Musk, Bill Gates, Jeff Bezos, and Mark Zuckerberg? Elon is more innovative, Bill is more of a trailblazer, Jeff is richer, and Mark is more influential—and younger to boot. This is purely conjecture, but Brian Chesky probably isn't staying up late at night considering how much better off he is than his high school quarterback; instead, he is more likely to compare himself to his own social circle, which is probably full of tech billionaires. In that company, even he might start feeling inadequate.

> **Facts & Figures: Brian Chesky**
> Born: 1981.
> Personal Net Worth: $4 billion.
> Occupation: CEO and Co-Founder of Airbnb (valued at $31 billion).
> Fanciest Title: In 2015, President Obama named him Ambassador of Global Entrepreneurship.

To prove his point, Malcolm Gladwell looked at research done across individuals who were pursuing degrees in science, technology, engineering, and mathematics ("STEM"). The results were consistent from Harvard down to community colleges: the top third of each class got over half of the degrees, the middle third got 20-30% of the degrees, and the bottom third got less than 20%. What does this mean? It means that the bottom two thirds of STEM students consistently dropped out—and at least some of those people had to have done so because they felt they couldn't measure up to their cohort. And this was true at Harvard just as at Hartwick (the example used in the presentation, which was ranked 165th in best liberal arts colleges in 2017-2018)—there was no special immunity for the brightest students.

As Malcolm puts it, "So what's happening at Harvard then? The kid in the bottom third of his class at Harvard does not say rationally: 'I'm in the 99.99th percentile of all students in the world when it comes to native math ability,' even though that's true. What that kid says is: 'Johnny over there is getting all the answers right and I'm not. I feel like I'm really stupid and I can't handle math so I'm going to drop out, get a fine arts degree, move to Brooklyn, work, make $15,000 a year and break my parents' heart, right?'" And that's true even though you could probably take any individual from the bottom third of Harvard, put them in a less competitive school, and they would likely graduate in the top third of their new class.

This is not an anomaly unique to graduation rates. Malcolm also examined the number of papers published by Ph.D. economists in the six years following their graduation. One would assume that anyone who had graduated from a top university would publish more articles due to the higher quality of education. Except, that doesn't happen; instead, we see a very similar pattern but with even more staggering results.

Economists that were in the 99th percentile of their class at a prestigious university (Harvard, Yale, M.I.T., Princeton, University of Chicago, etc.) published four to five articles. Economists in the 85th percentile published an average of around one paper, and those in the 55th percentile published less than one (*i.e.*, most published only one or none at all). So even well after graduation, the geniuses of geniuses still feel an inferiority complex and feel like they are "not good enough" to publish more.

Let's look at non-top-tier (top 30) schools. You might assume that a 99th-percentile student at a less prestigious university would publish less than the best students from the most elite schools. You would be correct, but the difference is minor: those at the top of non-top-tier universities are still publishing three to four papers in the six years following graduation. That means that some students from schools like

Boston University are publishing three times as much as 85th-percentile students from schools like Harvard.

So, what do Malcolm's insights get us? It turns out that, no matter how intelligent we are, we are all susceptible to feelings of inadequacy. From the outside, you might prefer to be in the top fifth of the class at Yale, but your outcome might be better if you were in the top one percent of your state school. That's because, if you only stay in your limited environment, like a child in the womb you will think that your immediate surroundings are the whole world. I'm not arguing that Ivy League students that just miss the top of their class should transfer to the nearest community college. But one simple way to rebuild your confidence—or find whole new reasons to believe in yourself—is to break out of that artificially small world and that constricted mindset through the wonders of travel.

Souvenirs

- Those at the top don't compare themselves to those at the bottom—they compare themselves to others at the top, for better and for worse.
  - Try to recognize when your sampling bias is getting you down. If you can notice it, you can change your narrative.
- People at the top of their class—regardless of the university—publish five times as much as at those at the bottom. People

at the bottom—regardless of the university—drop out much more frequently than those at the top.

- ○ If you feel like the biggest failure in an elite environment, you're probably not doomed, but you might want to get yourself a new backdrop, a new environment where you can stand out and feel the confidence you need to succeed.

Getting Around

Lack of experience and fear prevent many of us from becoming confident. They stand in the way of us becoming who we should be, the best versions of ourselves, capable and aware of our capabilities. There are a lot of ways to get to confidence. The most direct is to face your fears head on, do what you're uncertain of, and let yourself realize, "Hey, that wasn't that bad," and "If I did it once, I can do it again, and I can be better." The reason I've repeated that travel can be your cheat is because it gives you permission to fail. By putting you in a new environment, travel can remove some of the anxiety and stress that you attach to the fears you have to deal with on a regular basis.

Each of the stories that we've explored in this chapter addresses something different that falls under the greater umbrella of confidence. Michael's story showed us how we can use travel to build our *self-assurance* by finding an environment to practice and hone our skills. Jessica's story demonstrated how an unfortunate event spurred her to find the *courage* to change her career and achieve a work-life balance that she didn't know was possible. And finally Malcolm highlighted how important *self-esteem* is not only at school but in all aspects of life.

Each of these traits is valuable on its own, but when you have all three, you have the highest likelihood to go far in your life. After all, you could be very brave but have a negative perception of yourself that would prevent you from aiming high; or you could really believe in yourself but be too afraid to take any chances in life.

Wayne Gretzky said it best: "You miss 100% of the shots you don't take." To maximize your chance of scoring you need to believe that you can make the shot, have the courage to try, and see yourself as the person that is best for the job.

Moving to new environments has the ability to build all of these traits. As discussed previously, by developing your perspective you can gain clarity about yourself and become more self-assured. Facing challenges and exploring builds your courage. And interacting with more people can develop your self-esteem.

Shirley Chisholm was the first black woman elected to the United States Congress. She was also the U.S.'s first black candidate for a major party's presidential nomination, and the first woman to run for the Democratic Party's presidential nomination. In short, she's an icon of American history, and her picture should be under the dictionary definition for "trailblazer." Although Shirley was born in New York, her parents sent her to live with her grandmother in Barbados as a child, to receive an education and to ease the financial burden on them during the Great Depression.

Shirley had the following to say about living in Barbados: "Those early years of my life on the island of Barbados gave me the spirit, gave to me the spunk that was necessary to challenge all of these age-old traditions. I was never afraid of anything; I was never afraid of anybody and today is the same way. I am not afraid of anything, I am not afraid of anybody. You're going to hear from me."

There's no way of knowing whether she would have made so much history without her time abroad, but it's clear she considered it foundational. How much strength and spirit are you missing out on developing by staying put?

Suggested Itinerary: Increasing Your Confidence

- If you are in school or are looking to make a career switch, get ahead by getting hands-on experience in the field.

- Try to get an internship—the sooner the better, as you can build on that for a better opportunity after.
- If you have the means, consider paying for the privilege of training by enrolling in a class or program relating to your chosen career.

- Increase your confidence by doing new things. Even if this doesn't translate directly to your dream job, it's valuable just to know that you can handle yourself in unfamiliar situations.
  - When an interviewer asks why you think you'll be good at this job you can say, "I've done it already" or "I have a lot of experience picking up new things quickly, and in high-pressure environments."

- Things aren't always going to go to plan. If you have the strength to push through tough times, you have the strength to rebuild.

- If you're feeling unsuccessful, look deeper—how are you defining success? Are you comparing yourself to the wrong peer group?
  - Take a trip to meet more people, and step out of your current circle to evaluate yourself on a global scale rather than the bubble you've built around yourself.

PART 2

THE TRAVELER'S TOOL SET

DESTINATION 4

NEW SKILLS

———

"The more you learn, the less you fear. 'Learn' not in the sense of academic study, but in the practical understanding of life."
—JULIAN BARNES, *THE SENSE OF AN ENDING*

Roadmap

Let's get the obvious out of the way: yes, you can learn a new language, a sport, maybe even how to brew alcohol in your bathtub. These kinds of things all happen when you practice intentional travel. You can even make learning the focus of your travel, which will be covered more extensively in Destination 8, on traveling to study. But this chapter will primarily deal with how to acquire new skills while traveling for work or leisure.

Travel necessarily teaches us new skills because we are put in novel situations and shown new things. Experience is the best teacher. Period. You can read every single book ever written on basketball, but if you've never picked up a ball in your life then you'll lose to the experienced player who's never even picked up a book.

There's an entire religion that believes in this point. Like many religions, Mormonism finds new converts through missionary work by its members. However, Mormons stand out in the extent of their mission work. At any given moment, there are usually over 70,000 Mormons on missions in over 400 locations around the globe.

What does a mission look like? Two years abroad, trying to convert the local community to Mormonism. The missionaries have no choice as to where they are sent, and they live in conditions similar to the locals. They work with a partner, but are only allowed to call their family twice a year. And missionaries don't get paid for their work; in fact, many Mormons save up beforehand in order to support themselves for this period.

Unless you're out of touch with modern religious demographics, you probably already know that there aren't millions of new Mormons every year. In fact, most missionaries only convert a couple of people *per year*. That's two years of work, unpaid, away from your family and your home, with a success rate barely above zero. So why do Mormons invest so much in missions? Well, at least in part because spreading Mormonism is *not* the only point of missions. The mission also serves as a way to challenge young adults and prepare them for the difficulties of adulthood.

Over the course of their service, missionaries proselytize for ten or more hours per day, six days a week. They learn new languages, presentation skills, social skills, and more. They learn about other communities and what makes them tick. They learn how to rely on themselves. They learn about facing challenges, rejections, and failure. This is invaluable experience—even Mitt Romney, despite his family's wealth, was living in cramped quarters with three roommates during his mission in France.

Learning new skills takes hard work, but travel is the best teacher you could ask for.

Top Sights

Where in the World Is Vincent Sandiego?

"Every country's system has its own merit, you need to learn from all of the cultures that you experience and pull out the tool that you need in a given situation."

—VINCENT LIEW

Vincent Liew is currently the Global Executive Director at Boldface Hospitality; previously, he served as CEO for Wilson Associates, the world's third-largest hospitality design and solution company. Vincent comes from a very unorthodox background. Born and raised in Malaysia to Chinese parents, he received his education in England, and has experience running several large organizations in Hong Kong (Deloitte, WPP, and Aedas) and in the United States.

From very early in his life, Vincent has been influenced by his travels, and each culture he's experienced has taught him diverse life lessons that he carries with him to this day. In fact, he attributes a lot of his success to the broad exposure that he has had over the course of his life.

Vincent follows the credo, "Think global, act local." Mindful travel is a big part of working toward that goal. To this day, Vincent continues to take in the new knowledge that he encounters in every country that he visits. These lessons were vital for him to gain and succeed in positions of power in global organizations. Not only has he lived in many different countries, but Vincent has also worked in many different organizations abroad, which taught him how to build client relationships and how to best lead people in different parts of the world.

Vincent has learned that there is no one right way to do business—it varies based on context, including geography. "In Asia, you listen more than you talk and have to be able to read between the lines. In the U.S., you often talk more than you listen and everyone is much more upfront with their intentions." For another example, Vincent noted, "If you look at companies in many parts of Asia, China in particular, you will notice that the Business Development department has much more personnel than in the U.S. or Europe. This is because those cultures require a lot of hand-holding to develop and maintain relationships. It is not uncommon for verbal agreements or even written contracts to be rescinded, so much more time and effort needs to be devoted to the clientele."

When he was at Wilson Associates, Vincent was the logical choice to lead the company: he had significant international experience that gave him the background necessary to address the needs of a company with offices in Asia, the

Middle East, Europe, and the U.S. For the last few years of his life, Vincent has needed to divide his time equally between the U.S., Europe, and Asia. "You need to be global in today's economy; there is no one way of doing business. What works for you in Dallas will possibly get you in trouble in Tokyo. The more you understand a country's culture and different perspectives, the less trouble you will have navigating the local environment."

According to Vincent, technical skills are more vital to junior employees, but those higher on the corporate ladder need more soft skills (things like communication, problem-solving, and adaptability) to get the job done. For Vincent, he was able to get a leg up on most of his peers because he was able to develop his local know-how and his soft skills early on because of his extensive travels. "No matter how much you read about it, you cannot fully comprehend the feeling of being in a particular place unless you are actually there." So if you are looking to stand out among your peers, he recommends that you start developing your skills as early as possible, including learning how to interact on a global level.

Souvenirs:

- Vincent Liew comes from a diverse background and makes a point of learning from all his travels; this helped elevate him to the top of his field early on.

- Make it a priority when traveling to take in the local know-how, observe how people work in that country, and figure out what type of leadership style is preferred.
- In general, you should focus on technical skills in the early part of your career, and soft skills for management positions later on. That said, soft skills can also give you a leg up from the beginning, so take whatever opportunities you can to develop them.

- Even though he's already at the top of the food chain, Vincent continues to soak up everything that he can to grow as a leader.
  - There are always new lessons to be learned, whether you're just starting out or you're a seasoned veteran. Every experience is a learning experience, whether it's as general as how to be a better leader or as specific as how much effort to put into relationship management in China.

Aloha, Hawaii / Aloha, New York

"My life lesson [from travel] is you can't be afraid of the unknown; you have to take life by the horns and always advance forward."

—JERRY WANG

You're on a beach. The sun is shining, the waves are crashing, and you're surrounded by friends and loved ones. This sounds like a great vacation, except it's not a vacation.

Jerry Wang grew up in Honolulu, Hawaii—most people's dream getaway. Unsurprisingly, a lot of his family and friends still live there, but not Jerry.

On spring break during his junior year of high school, Jerry took a two-week trip to New York City to visit his uncle. His uncle showed him everything that New York had to offer: he took him to the stock exchange, introduced him to his friends who were lawyers and bankers, and showed him the big-city (rather than big-island) lifestyle.

It was Jerry's first time experiencing something different from the laid-back vibes of Hawaii.

"I always felt like there was something missing in my life growing up in Hawaii, but didn't know what it was. I loved my friends and my family, but often times I would look up at the stars and wonder if there was something more. Sometimes fate interjects coincidences into your life that set you on a completely new journey. As a young and impressionable teenager, that trip to New York was the spark that sent me on a new vector."

On the plane ride back, he wrote down his game plan in his journal:

1. Go to school on the east coast.
2. Get into banking.
3. Crush it.

That plan would set the tone for the next fifteen years of his life… and he did manage to "crush it." At only 33 years old, Jerry is already a Principal in The Carlyle Group, one of the largest private equity and alternative investment firms in the world, but as Jerry would tell you, there were a few more steps between getting into the finance industry and thriving in it. What helped him make the leap was the mindset he gained through travel and brought back to Wall Street.

I neglected to mention at the beginning of this story that Jerry is one of my closest friends. I was best man at his wedding and it has been my privilege to see him work so hard to get to where he is. Hardly a week goes by that we don't speak to or see each other.

Jerry is also the person that I've traveled with the most. We have had the good fortune of visiting dozens of countries together. That means I've had a front row seat for the transformation those travels have wrought in him. I can recall countless lessons we learned together: simple things like learning negotiation from haggling on the streets of Asia to the wisdom of how to spot scammers trying to take advantage of two American tourists in more countries than I can name. I'm proud to have shared these experiences with Jerry. I'm glad we've grown into smarter, better, and more mature people, together.

Jerry says, "Traveling gave me a more robust way of looking at different problems, different issues, understanding what they are and attacking those issues from unconventional angles. Experiencing different cultures, your mindset has to be an open door that invites new possibilities."

The uncle that first inspired Jerry in New York has since moved back to China to take over his family's medical device business. But he has become a mentor to Jerry, who continues to visit him. These visits aren't vacations; in fact, they're often busier than most people's full-time job schedules. "I'd work with him the entire week I'm back [in China]. Typically, the days are packed with back-to-back meetings six days a week. We get up at eight in the morning and work until nine and then have dinner typically with clients. We typically get back around twelve or one, and then rinse and repeat."

Jerry credits these trips with teaching him the importance of the human element in business. Rather than see business as a zero-sum game, he came to see that business relationships are still relationships: both sides need to benefit, or the arrangement falls apart.

Like Vincent before him, Jerry learned that deals in China are not as clear-cut as they are in the States: "Almost everything is done with a handshake after the meeting." He carried these lessons that he learned there to apply to his everyday life back in the States. Jerry leverages his experience to develop real connections with the executives of his portfolio companies, rather than stick to the formalities. "Beyond just a lender or an investor, I am really trying to bring a partnership to them."

By changing the way he looks at these relationships, Jerry was able to really listen and connect. "If you just have a conversation, versus a Q&A session, then you can develop a respect for each other and a mutual understanding. ... The earlier you realize that an investment is a living, breathing company and it's run by living, breathing people that have their own dreams and anxieties, the more insights you can glean."

Souvenirs:

- Although he grew up living someone's dream in Hawaii, Jerry Wang realized that he wanted to emulate his uncle, a businessman in New York.
  - There are few things in life as valuable as a good mentor or teacher. If you find someone living the life you want, observe and take in as much as you can from them.

- Jerry's trips to visit family in China taught him the value of developing business relationships, a realization vital to getting ahead in his industry.
  - Both empathy and relationship-building are skills that take time to develop. Traveling helps train both, because seeing how people and relationships differ in other places can fill you in on what you need to know.
  - The sooner you realize that everyone that you interact with has a life of their own, the better relationships you'll be able to build.

From Peace Corps to Biz Corps

"If you don't grapple with why you do things this way versus that way, you'll never change. Travel is a way to expand your view on business and how things can be done differently."

—COLIN DEFFET

Hollywood gives you a funny idea of what working life is like. Until someone disillusions you, you could be forgiven for thinking that most people in business travel the world on private jets, drinking freely and somehow rolling in the big bucks. For most people, their first job is more likely to take them to a windowless conference room than a scenic vista.

Colin Deffet found himself in a similar situation after he graduated from the University of South Carolina over a decade ago. "You graduate college at 22 and you are probably really ignorant to what the job market is going to look like. I had the perception that I was going to get a really cool job where I travel the world right off the bat; but to no surprise most jobs did not have much travel and involved me spending all of my time at a desk."

Colin wanted a job that would develop his skills in management and continue to improve his Spanish proficiency, because in college he had majored in international business operations and minored in Spanish, but he didn't want a typical desk job. He wanted real, meaningful experience. Finding something that fit the bill for a first job wasn't easy, but Colin was lucky enough to have had an uncle who had been in the Peace Corps. On his uncle's recommendation, Colin decided to join as well, working on small-business development in Guatemala.

Facts & Figures: Peace Corps

Formed: 1961 by President John F. Kennedy.

Volunteers: Nearly 220,000 Americans in 141 countries.

Film Appearances: Featured as a plot device in *Airplane!*, *Christmas with the Kranks*, and *Shallow Hal*.

"In Guatemala, my ego shrunk, my patience grew, and I learned to appreciate connections more. Those are all things that apply to any environment, but especially in business. You become curious and you are sincerely asking a question versus just filling ear space. I genuinely like to connect, and these are things that people appreciate as an ambassador for my organization and country. Those are skills that can be appreciated anywhere in the world."

In addition to all these concrete skills, his time in Guatemala opened Colin up to see new possibilities outside of the desk jobs. He used the experience to leverage his way to do consulting work on four continents, working with companies like Enterprise Solutions to Poverty, OPIC, and FINTRAC.

"Living somewhere is different than traveling somewhere because you spend more time building relationships and pondering why people do things the way that they do it. They give you different outlooks on life and time. The longer you spend somewhere the more you realize the way they do things may be right or they may be wrong. You hold yourself up to a light and you start to understand yourself better because you start to compare yourself and how you do things versus how other people do things."

Currently, Colin works at Allied Mineral Products, a leading producer of monolithic refractory products (feel free to google what that means) in its International Sales department. In this role, Colin is directly responsible for sales and strategy in Central America, the Caribbean, and parts of South America.

The job description was considerably less exciting when he first got it, but Colin leveraged his knowledge of the region to identify new opportunities for his company. "I was willing to travel to what many consider the edge of the world. I pushed business in places that were difficult to get to and most didn't want to go to."

During his time searching for new potential sales, Colin saw that there was significant opportunity to work with sugar mills and other biomass fuel power generation companies. Most of these businesses were located in Mexico, Colombia, and—you guessed it—Guatemala. Colin used his experience from the Peace Corps to jump-start his efforts in the region. He also took the time to learn his clients' processes to identify how best he could add value. Because of the initiative he showed and the experience he leveraged, Colin is now considered the expert on sugar mills.

"The more times you parachute into a country, the more times you feel out of place and uncomfortable, the better you are at navigating when you're out of your comfort zone. ... It's kind of similar to joining the NBA from college basketball, at first things move really fast but after a season or two things start to slow down."

Colin's insights led me to an interesting question. Why doesn't the company hire more onsite people to go after new business in the local market? According to Colin, "It shows a different level of commitment when a company sends someone from headquarters to talk and demonstrate the interest in their business. If they never talk to anyone that is American, then why would they do business with a company that is headquartered in Columbus, Ohio?"

Colin's logic is sound. When I worked in mergers and acquisitions, we often employed the same strategy to court various businesses to potentially buy out. While local leadership was the first line, we would often bring corporate leadership (CEO, CFO, etc.) along on pitches to demonstrate that we truly valued the business as part of the greater business of our company, not just a regional concern.

Souvenirs:

- Rather than resign himself to a desk job, Colin joined the Peace Corps after college, with a focus on business development.
  - For college students that want to continue learning in another setting, the Peace Corps and other international

service organizations are excellent opportunities to build skills, get experience abroad, and come out with a great nest egg.

- At his latest job, Colin used his knowledge of Latin America to identify new opportunities and develop his own niche within the company.
  - If you don't like a structure, get out of it. Learning and skill development happen outside of the normal, and outside of your comfort zone.
  - If you can develop skills and figure out how to apply them, you may be able to adjust your role to better suit your passions.

Getting Around

Author, motivational speaker, and consultant Simon Sinek believes, "The single most important quality of leadership is curiosity. And so those who are curious about others and curious about the world, it only benefits you in everything else you do." To travel is to develop your sense of curiosity toward and engagement with the world. And the more curious you are, the more likely you are to try to figure things out, or specifically to learn whatever it is you have to learn to satisfy your curiosity.

As Colin has demonstrated, you don't have to be stuck in the role you came into. He was able to use his expertise to make a job more suited to his skills and more profitable for his employer. If you're interested in making travel a part of your job, it might be a good idea to become an expert on wherever you'd like to travel; that way, you have a better idea of why sending you there for work could be beneficial.

Colin's skills came from immersing himself deeply in one culture, but Vincent built his career in part based on the breadth of his travels. In both of these stories, traveling brought the opportunity to examine other cultures and figure out how to adapt.

A study by Philip L. Pearce and Faith Foster looked at self-reported learning achievements of backpackers: more than 62% of respondents said they developed or improved in twenty generic skills, and 35% of respondents said they improved 42 generic skills. These generic skills included management of time and resources, effective communication, decision-making, and patience—so, exactly the kinds of soft skills that most of us need to succeed.

Survival of the fittest is a funny thing. People often misinterpret the phrase to mean that the most fit, i.e., the strongest, will survive. But really, the question of fit is about fitting *in* to changing environments. When things are different, can you learn the new skills necessary to make it work? That adaptability is the reason you have thumbs and don't have a tail. But staying in one place means you'll only ever develop the skills you need to survive in that environment, and you might be left behind when that environment shifts. The more environments you expose yourself to, the more other things you'll have to learn, and the more likely you'll be able to stand out and thrive wherever you end up.

Suggested Itinerary: Acquiring New Skills

- Anyone that you meet in your life has the potential to teach you something new. You never know who will make a lifelong mentor, or who will be a valuable education in what not to do.
  - Go out and find as many teachers as you can.
- Immersive experiences are the best way to pick up new skills quickly, and practically.
  - Trying to learn a new language? Surround yourself in it, and speak nothing else.
- Travel can also promote a host of soft skills, like decision-making and time management.
  - As Mormons know, immersive cultural experiences can teach young adults to grow up fast, learning responsibility and resilience.
  - Solo travel, or travel with little contact back home, also improves your confidence and self-reliance.
- If your job involves working with a certain region, spending time there can give you a leg up on your business.
  - Take a work or a personal trip to feel the pulse of the area and its people.

DESTINATION 5

WELLNESS

"Health is a state of complete physical, mental and social well-being, and not merely the absence of disease or infirmity."

—WORLD HEALTH ORGANIZATION

Roadmap

Unless you've been living in an underground bomb shelter for the last few decades (did anyone else love *Blast from the Past?*), you've probably heard a lot about wellness. In many ways, people are more aware of the importance of health than ever. It seems like there's a new fad diet, workout, and secret trick to "A Better You!" every week. A lot of it is probably scams and bunk, but the sentiment behind it is excellent: it's worth putting time and effort into making sure you feel good.

The older you get, the more you may realize that well-being is not a guarantee. Health is something you have to work at to build and maintain.

Travel can help with that. People know that taking a vacation is good for you, but not enough are aware of how bad it can be *not* to take a break. One study found that "vacationing every year reduced the overall risk of death by about 20 percent, and the risk of death from heart disease by as much as 30 percent." Another study noted that women who take vacations once every six years are eight times more likely to get a heart attack than those who take two vacations per year. Tell that to your boss the next time they ask you to cancel your trip out of town to work all weekend.

Of course, physical health is only one aspect of wellness; just as important is your mental well-being. When wellness has come up throughout *The Traveler's Edge*, it's largely in this latter capacity: the ways in which travel makes you reassess your priorities, listen to yourself, and find a balance that actually works. But travel is also good for you in very concrete, physical ways; it promotes activities that are good for your body, making you excited to do the things that you might neglect in your daily routine (walking around, spending time outside, catching up on sleep), and inspiring you to change. In this chapter, we will explore more stories on how travel can lead to healthier habits for your body and mind.

Top Sights

Kicking Back Some Muay Thai

"This is it… my last hurrah."

I remember the thought crossing my mind as I pressed "buy" on an open-ended ticket to Thailand. I was going to be traveling alone for the first time in my life, so I had no idea whether I would want to come back in a week or brave staying away for the full month that I was aiming for. I was 22 years old and I had just spent the previous three months traveling across the globe for the best summer of my life (at that point).

**

Does this sound familiar?

It should. This is the first story that I shared at the start of our journey. But I didn't tell you the full tale. This trip was my first exposure to experiential travel, and it became the foundation upon which I built the last decade of my life. So let's pick up where we left off.

**

I had traveled before, but never like this. Not only was my time in Thailand going to be the longest I would be away from home by myself, but I was doing it to train in Muay Thai, a sport in which I had no previous experience. Honestly, it started on a whim. I had six weeks until my first full-time job after college, and I wanted to do something different. I bought my ticket using airline miles at 4 a.m. on a Wednesday in early September. I was on a plane five days later. I think my parents thought I was in a drunken stupor when I decided to do the trip, but they figured I had to grow up some time. So off I went.

Facts & Figures: Muay Thai

Established: Mid-1700s.

Also Known As: Thai Boxing, or The Art of Eight Limbs (fists, elbows, knees, and shins).

Choice Moves: Superman punch, spinning elbow, reverse roundhouse kick.

After one of the longest string of flights I've ever had the displeasure of flying (New York → Hong Kong → Bangkok → Phuket), I emerged from a propeller plane red-eyed and drenched in stale sweat. It was late, but there were plenty of cabs. I gave the driver the name of my training camp. I watched as the city disappeared in the rearview mirror.

After about thirty minutes of driving, the taxi stopped and backed up to follow a path down a hill I hadn't even noticed. I was at my new home.

I roamed around without a clue, hoping that someone would still be awake at 2 a.m. so I could get a few hours of rest before my first training at 6 a.m. I stumbled upon an employee sleeping in the open-air gym (I didn't ask why), and after some brief confusion, I was led to my lodging: a 10' x 15' room with a bed, a dresser, a ceiling fan, a gas stove with a wok, and a mini-fridge that looked older than I was.

The next four weeks of my life would follow the same schedule: up at 6 a.m. to run a 5k around the jungle; two hours working out barefoot on a concrete floor (jumping a weighted rope, hitting heavy bags, and sparring with people 30 pounds lighter than I was, who knocked all the air out of my lungs with ease), a break for lunch and rest, and another three hours of training after. There was no air conditioning. There was no water fountain. There was a fighting ring, and bags to hit, and people to hit you.

It was excruciating. It was also the happiest I'd ever been. I've been an athlete most of my life, which at that point meant I had never missed a season of sports while I went to school, but this was on a completely different level. There was no after school, no mom and dad, and no pizza parties. I didn't get a break just because I was new; in fact, I had a bloody ear on my first day from a close punch.

Many in the camp barely spoke a word of English (why would they?). I had traveled to places where I didn't know the language before, and I had even studied American Sign Language, but I never realized just how much people can understand each other even without a common language. I made friends with others in the camp, but I also became more comfortable spending time on my own. In college, I always felt out of place if I had to eat lunch by myself, and considered myself lonely if I didn't have plans to go drinking on the weekend. Training changed that. I didn't have the luxury to be hungover the next morning. I cut down on drinking, and replaced that voice that screamed of FOMO (fear of missing out) in my head with one that reminded me what time I had to wake up. I started to appreciate hanging out with myself and being in the present moment, rather than worrying about other people and what I was going to do next.

When I came back, my body was a patchwork of scabs and bruises. My parents said I looked like I'd returned from a war zone. But my face was smiling. My mind was calm. My outlook was sunny. The bruises would fade, and underneath them I was in the best shape of my life. I was beyond happy with my experience; I had found an activity that I still love today, which helps me to de-stress and feel good.

I did it again the next year. I brought some friends with me, too, but I still took plenty of time for myself.

Souvenirs:

- On a whim, I went on a month-long solo trip to Thailand to train in a martial art.
    - If you have the room for it in your life, lean into your whims. Things don't have to be the result of laborious decision-making processes in order to be worthwhile. Sometimes, a whim is your subconscious suggesting you might need something you're not used to needing. Listen.
- I put myself in an extreme environment where I had no one to depend on except myself. It helped me develop healthier habits, and made me comfortable in my own skin and my own head.
    - Just as with developing new skills, the best way to drill better habits (whether that's working out, or feeling more at ease being alone) into yourself is through immersive experiences.

The Four-Hour Metamorphosis

"Though you can upgrade you brain domestically, traveling and relocating provides unique conditions that make progress much faster."

—TIM FERRISS

In June 2010, I was at JFK airport about to embark on a two-week trip to South Africa for the World Cup. I remember having a few beers in my system when a bright orange and red cover with palm trees grabbed my attention from the airport newsstand. The book was *The 4-Hour Workweek* by Tim Ferriss. The subtitle read, *Escape 9-5, Live Anywhere, and Join The New Rich.* My brain flashed, "Here, take my money!" Like many people, I was enamored with the idea that you don't have to work like a dog to be successful. I was 25, still not very familiar with the concept of working smart instead of working hard. Needless to say I bought the book. Good marketing. Bravo, Tim. Bravo.

If you've never heard of Tim Ferriss, he's the direct result of one crazy ride of a life. Here are a few highlights: he nearly failed kindergarten; he did a year in Japan as an exchange student; he dropped out of Princeton; he tried to start a gym chain in Taiwan only to be shut down by Triads (a gang); he went back to Princeton; he quit a job where he made $40,000 per year to start a nutrition company where he earned the same every month; he burnt himself out; and then he took a vacation and meant to travel for a month, but ended up doing it for a year and a half (yep, we're going to talk about that last part). That's a lot, and it's also just skimming the surface. Today, Tim is an author, podcast host, and entrepreneur.

In early 2004, Tim was killing it with his company, but the company was also killing him. "I was miserable and overworked... I needed a recharge and four weeks seemed 'reasonable' by whatever made-up benchmark you can use for such a thing." So Tim took a vacation. He decided to do a little experiment while he was at it. He wanted to try to have as little involvement with his business as possible during his vacation. Tim had just learned about Pareto's Law, which says that 80% of effects come from 20% of causes. He took a look at his business and realized that just five of his 120 clients yielded more than 95% of his revenue; on the other hand, it was largely a few small clients that were giving him the issues that took so much out of his life. So he let go of the small, misery-inducing clients, and concentrated on the big guns.

Meanwhile, he lost the thread of taking a "reasonable" vacation. "[I] decided that I deserve a full three months to explore my roots in Scandinavia after four weeks in Spain. If there were any real time bombs or pending disasters, they would certainly crop up in the first four weeks, so there really wasn't any additional risk in extending my trip to three months." He turned out to be right. In fact, as he spent an additional fourteen months traveling the world, his business was thriving. He came home to teach a class at Princeton on the lessons he learned, and then turned that class into his bestselling book.

Tim continues to have crazy travel adventures to this day. He's written more bestsellers, and invested in and advised many companies you've heard of (Uber, Shopify, TaskRabbit). Not a bad return for doing less work than ever.

Souvenirs:

- Tim Ferriss's business was doing well, but he wasn't. He decided to take time off to travel and to let go of clients that were making him miserable.
  - No job is worth your well-being. It's your duty to yourself to prioritize your health; everything else can take a back seat. Don't wait for yourself to break before you start fixing things.
  - In addition to allowing yourself to take a step back, try to identify what your worst stressors are and, if possible, remove them.
- Tim became more successful than ever after he stopped overworking himself. He embraced the opportunity to keep traveling, and encouraged others to work smart (and less) too.
  - It's easy to convince yourself that being miserable is vital to keep your life going, but it shouldn't be the case. A healthier, happier person often does better work than a depressed, exhausted one.

Mindfulness Is Next to Godliness

"We can all take responsibility for our own minds. Our brains are constantly being shaped wittingly or unwittingly, most of the time our brains are being shaped unwittingly. We have an opportunity to take more responsibility for the intentional shaping of our own minds. ... Well-being is a skill."

—RICHARD DAVIDSON

Richard Davidson is a neuroscientist and the founder of the Center for Healthy Minds at the University of Wisconsin–Madison. You might have heard of him from the work he does with the Dalai Lama regarding the effects of meditation. Over the years, his center has done some really fascinating research on broader themes regarding emotional well-being. Professor Davidson and his colleagues are specifically interested in neuroplasticity, the brain's wiring, which affects adaptability. They contend that you can train your brain to be happy, just like you can train yourself to learn a new skill such as playing an instrument.

Professor Davidson writes, "Based on our research, well-being has four constituents that have each received serious scientific attention. Each of these four is rooted in neural circuits and each of these neural circuits exhibits plasticity—so we know that if we exercise these circuits, they will strengthen. Practicing these four skills can provide the substrate for enduring change, which can help to promote higher levels of well-being in our lives."

The four constituent parts that he refers to are resilience, outlook, attention, and generosity. (All of these things can be practiced while traveling; in fact, we've considered some of these concepts already. Jessica showed *resilience* after her break-up, Howard's *outlook* led him to believe in his ideas when Starbucks didn't, and mindful travel is all about using your *attention*. We'll be talking a lot about *generosity* in the chapter on spirituality.)

As with any skill, some of these take more time to develop than others, and can vary for different people. Resilience takes the longest time to develop, potentially requiring thousands of hours of mindful meditation before you'll see noticeable results. This makes sense, since resilience is about how long it takes you to recover from adversity, and rewiring how you react to bad situations is a serious undertaking. The other three constituents take less time: for example, an average of seven hours of practice over the course of two weeks improving your outlook (how positive you perceive things to be) will show results in your brain circuitry.

So, what does this look like in practice? There are different meditations that are best suited for different constituents, but we can start with a basic one. For working on your resilience and attention, let's have a brief, grossly oversimplified lesson in **mindful meditation**. This book has talked a lot about mindfulness; using mindfulness with meditation rather than (or preferably in addition to) travel can get you some of the same results, including the ability to focus on and appreciate what is around you.

So try this: sit down. Focus on your breath. When your mind starts to wander (and it will), don't bother scolding yourself. Just bring yourself back to focusing on your breath. Do this for ten minutes, and then try doing it for longer. That's it! Nothing fancy required. Though you could wear a cool robe if you want to; no judgments here.

Souvenirs:

- Professor Richard Davidson's studies on emotional well-being have concluded that we can train our minds to be more emotionally healthy. He has identified four constituents that can be improved to help us live happier and fuller lives: resilience, outlook, attention, and generosity.
  - You can train the way you think in order to be a happier person. That's science!
- Professor Davidson advocates for mindful meditation (and the Dalai Lama agrees) to find a happier you.

○ Give mindful meditation a try. The basic version just requires taking time to focus on your breath; once you've mastered that, refer to the good professor for more.

Getting Around

According to Lonely Planet, Wellness Tourism is "the industry's fastest growing sector, with a 10% rise this year making it a plus $500 billion market." It's great that people are concentrating on their well-being, but I wonder if wellness tourism should even need its own category. All tourism has the potential to be wellness tourism. One person's high-end spa is another person's surfing trip is another person's gourmet food tour; wellness doesn't mean the same thing to everyone, but you can find your flavor of it however you travel.

As Tim Ferriss learned, success doesn't matter if you lack the well-being to enjoy it. That's probably what the Roman poet Virgil meant when he wrote, "The greatest wealth is health." Just as people put hours every day into building their wealth, so too should you devote yourself to building your wellness. Professor Davidson suggests you can become a happier you with mindful meditation; or you can do what I did and drill better habits into yourself by jumping head-first into an activity that will whip your brain and body into fighting shape.

Regardless of what road you take, travel is there to help accelerate your betterment. If you're stressed out at work, it may be hard for you to get over that stress just sitting at your desk. Have you ever woken up feeling fine, only to feel a knot in your chest the moment you think of what you have to do at the office? Have you felt fine and dandy outside, but noticed your mood shift to anger and resentment the moment the elevator opens onto your company's floor? The human brain has a function called episodic memory formation; basically, you associate certain feelings with the places and times you felt them. There's probably a very good reason why you haven't wanted to go back to the coffee shop where your ex gave you an "it's not you, it's me" speech.

But it's not as simple to avoid your workplace as it is that bar where you bombed karaoke one time. Traveling is a simple way to put yourself in a different place and remove that extra obstacle, allowing you to build healthy habits on a level playing field. When you get back home, you'll have a jump start on integrating those better routines into your daily life. Voila.

That and George's patented muscle-building wristwatch (only four easy payments of $99.99 if you call in the next five seconds!) are all you need for A Better You.

Suggested Itinerary: Improving Your Wellness

- Not only can taking a vacation make you happy, *not* taking time off may cause drastic results on your health. So take a break!
- The best way to build many new healthy habits is to immerse yourself in a radically different lifestyle.
- Your work should not be at the expense of your mental or physical health. If it is, try to assess and cut out your biggest stressors; focus in on what is working, and give yourself permission to step away when you need to.
- Train your brain to be happy. Stretch those neurons by practicing mindful meditation.
    - Focus on activities that make you more resilient, improve your outlook, increase your attention, and inspire your generosity.
    - Remember, you're more likely to be able to train yourself in these new habits if you remove yourself from the stressors of your daily life.

DESTINATION 6

NETWORK

———

"What you've done becomes the judge of what you're going to do—especially in other people's minds. When you're traveling, you are what you are right there and then. People don't have your past to hold against you. No yesterdays on the road."

—WILLIAM LEAST HEAT-MOON, *BLUE HIGHWAYS*

Roadmap

Networking. A lot of people probably have a shiver go down their spine when they hear that word. For me, it always represented a chore that I needed to do but didn't really want to. It can feel forced and disingenuous. To some, it is the act of interacting with someone because you want something from them. If you're confused by what I'm talking about, you might be one of the fortunate few that never had to witness friends and strangers form a circle around someone with status as if they were praying to a deity.

I am not a naturally social person, I grew up very shy. As a child I lived in three very different countries with different cultures and languages; it took me a long time to feel comfortable enough to break out of my shell. Unfortunately, there is no trick to socializing that I've learned over the years. You just have to do it. Networking can be uncomfortable, especially if you haven't done a lot of it. It helps, sometimes, to remember that other people are just as uncomfortable as you are. Or maybe they're not, and they're experts at this, and you can just copy whatever they're doing. Either way, it'll be fine.

Let's not focus on the bad or the awkward. In this chapter, let's think about networking from its many enjoyable angles, because it *can* be enjoyable. It's not wrong to say that networking is just a formal way of making friends. Plus, the reason people do it (even when they don't want to) is because the end result is great—i.e., there will be more people to care about you, to guide you, to mentor you, and to push you to succeed. So let's examine how to use travel to develop your network, and how and why travel can strengthen your existing network.

Top Sights

Home Is Everywhere Your Friends Are

"Has [my job] expanded my network? Absolutely. Am I meeting people who I wouldn't necessarily spend time with outside of my day-to-day? Absolutely. Is it making me culturally see things from a different perspective? Yes."

—JULIA

When she was in college, Julia decided to head back home early from a trip to Spain. She was flying standby from Madrid, and although she initially got a seat on the day's only flight home, she was asked to give up that seat shortly after she boarded because the flight was oversold.

But Julia wasn't the only one asked to give up her seat. She ended up making friends with the other standby travelers who had been so unceremoniously dumped, and the entire group spent an excellent day together in Madrid before returning the next day to catch the following flight.

Seven years later, Julia was looking for a roommate for graduate school. In the Facebook group for her incoming class, she saw a post from someone else looking for a roommate. She recognized the face immediately: it was one of her standby friends from Spain. The two were joyfully reunited and lived together for the next two years. They remain extremely close to this day.

Julia's trip taught her a valuable lesson: never underestimate the power of socializing, even when you're far from home. You can never anticipate the effect that a chance meeting will have on you years down the line.

Today, Julia works at one of the top consulting companies in the world. Travel is most of her job description. There's hardly a week that she isn't on one airplane on Monday morning, and on another one coming home on Thursday afternoon. Julia lives in New York, but has projects all around the U.S., so she bounces between the coasts and everywhere in between. She's also traveled a lot internationally outside of work.

Because of her experience in Spain, Julia has been inspired to be more proactive in expanding her social circle. And Julia has combined that sociability with her work travel to create an extensive network. Every time she visits a new city, she makes it known to her social network that she'd love to hear advice from any locals. If she doesn't know any locals personally, she asks friends for introductions. As she says, "Part of building a network is going where you don't know anyone." She then strengthens tenuous connections and maintains strong ones by making plans with whomever she knows every time she's in their area, and keeping in touch even when she's not. "I take the time to reach out to people that I haven't talked to in a while. Just to check in [to] see how they are doing. That often leads to, 'Let's do a trip together' or 'Let's do something.' And I actually do it. I think people say a lot of things and don't follow through."

By her own admission, it's a lot of work to maintain such a large web of friends and acquaintances. But to her, it's routine—like going to the gym or flossing. You simply need to take time to catch up with people regularly, and then make a point of pulling out your mental rolodex every time you travel. Over the years, this practice has yielded some very worthwhile dividends. Some people have a hard time getting friends to go out to a bar with them. Julia could probably send a few emails and have three friends meet her for a night out in Berlin, and a fourth local friend willing to host all of them.

For the record, there isn't a week that Julia doesn't reach out to see how I am doing. She is absolutely true to her principles but I also know that she actually cares about every single person in her network. She's also the go-to person everyone in our social circle reaches out to when they're trying to hang out as a group or plan a party. I am not saying these points to give needless praise (you're great, Julia!); rather,

I am highlighting this to show that it is possible to be an ace networker and a genuine friend.

The benefits of being well connected aren't just social. Networking obviously has a business bent to it, and Julia has had many opportunities to grow her career because of her connections. When any of her many friends find themselves in a position to hire a consultant that they trust, Julia is at the top of their list. So much of business is about the people you work with day in and day out, and it's no surprise that people would rather work with someone they know to be approachable and smart. And most companies would love to have someone on their payroll who can bring in new clients from personal relationships.

Speaking from my own experience, another reason networking can come in handy has to do with the high stress of certain jobs. Working life is hard enough; add a turbulent travel schedule to the mix and it's easy to feel a little at sea. Building relationships in your work destinations can help, using friendly faces as an anchor to steady you. Working with, or taking breaks to see, people that you sincerely like can make long nights pass more quickly and tough assignments feel doable. At the very least, you get a sympathetic ear and a brief reprieve from everything on your plate. That simple relief can be just as valuable as the opportunities that come from being well connected.

Souvenirs:

- When Julia was flying standby back from Spain while she was in college, she made friends with fellow travelers. One of those travelers ended up becoming her roommate and friend almost a decade later.
  - The secret thing about networking is that people do it all the time accidentally; it can be as simple as being friendly in an unexpected situation.
- Now well aware of the power of networking, Julia uses her work travel as a consultant as an excuse to develop and maintain a broad network of friends and acquaintances.
  - If you have a stressful travel-heavy job, taking the time to develop relationships where you travel can ease the burden, and provide a benefit that outlasts your position.

Branding with Purpose

"For my six-month stint I went to six continents, eighteen countries. That was one of the most mindful trips that I have ever done. … It's really learning not so much from a broader cultural sense, but how does business and startup work in this [country]? So it was very interesting, completely different than any kind of travel I've done."

—PRISCILLA BABB

Priscilla Babb is half Chinese, one quarter Mexican, and one quarter white. Her diverse roots sparked an interest in traveling from an early age. But this story is not about that. Priscilla started an education non-profit with a classmate and the former Finance Minister of Taiwan while studying at Princeton. The non-profit, Global Compassion Project, takes American students from eleven to eighteen years old and helps them travel to China to teach English; in eleven years in operation, they've helped over 10,000 youths. But this story isn't about that project either.

This story is about what happened when Priscilla quit her job. In 2017, she was working in brand management for S.C. Johnson in Chicago, leading the Windex brand. She left without having her next job lined up; in fact, she didn't even know what industry or field she wanted to work in. "My only goal was to join a startup with a cause that I believed in."

But she did have a plan. Priscilla was never the type to wait until retirement to see the world; at that point, she'd already made two different trips around the globe, each over six months long. Over those trips she finally honed in on a method to not only see the world but also build skills, broaden her network, and make herself more valuable to employers.

So when she quit, she embarked on another adventure. This time, her focus wasn't beaches and ski slopes, but offices. She went networking and learning about startups all around the globe. "Over six months, I had picked out four or five anchor conferences within four or five cities, with one or two incubators or accelerators [in each]. I mapped out my friends in these areas and just went."

She left a lot of her time unplanned to leave room for suggestions or referrals that came through friends and people that she met on the trip. Having a loose schedule also had the added benefit of giving her time to take a break when needed. She also made sure to make time for *pro bono* work, which had unexpected benefits: "One of the easiest ways for me to meet people was I was doing a lot of *pro bono* work while abroad… If [startup companies] don't have the ability to pay for a marketing director or creative director, I would be happy to come in and brainstorm with them and talk branding."

Using a combination of existing connections, *pro bono* work, and networking at incubators and conferences, Priscilla ended up vetting over a hundred companies. She found that startups were very open to her emailing out of the blue, especially when she identified herself as coming from the U.S. and wanting to help and learn. She ended up working with dozens of companies, meeting scores of people, and traveling across six continents. At the end of this epic journey, Priscilla knew she had found the opportunity that excited her most for the next phase of her career. And that choice surprised her.

"I started at New York Fashion Week thinking I was going to go into luxury goods. [I] ended up at a biometric cyber security startup commercializing tech out of a leading academic institution." In all her time at tech conferences, she got the tech bug. Her travels led to her next gig in that field, and she's been happily working since.

Reentry did not come without its hiccups. Although Priscilla maintains that taking time off to travel is absolutely worthwhile, you have to be prepared for some questions when you get back. "Companies will ask you, 'What have you been doing?'" Some people will like and respect that you've traveled, but some will be skeptical. Priscilla says that this very concern is why she focused her latest trip on "building more purpose and marketability... it doesn't have to be a lot, it's just a quarter turn of being a little bit more mindful as opposed to 'I am just going to travel.'" Employers are often concerned about how long it's been since you've had the structure of a job in your life, but if you're able to show the structure you built for yourself and the skillset you worked up, you'll be a much more appealing candidate.

Souvenirs:

- Priscilla went on a trip around the world to grow her network, exchanging her skills in brand management for the opportunity to pick the brains of employees in different industries.

- Sometimes, life is like a box of chocolates. Don't know what you want? Get a sampler.
- Through her travels, Priscilla ended up finding a new job in a new industry that she loves.
  - When your skills are translatable to a lot of fields, you should take the time to consider new ways to apply them in the industry that you find most exciting and promising.
- In order to facilitate reentering the workforce, Priscilla emphasized the ways in which she structured her time away and the skills she honed in the meantime.
  - Although many companies value travel experience and want employees who have taken the time to figure out what they want, some may still give you a hard time for not being traditionally employed. Be prepared to articulate why your time off was as valuable, or more valuable, than traditional work experience.
- **Bonus:** If you want to be like Priscilla (who could blame you?), here's her very own suggested itinerary:
  - *Plan ahead.* Spanning whatever amount of time you can take off, pick several large startup conferences around the world. Make a travel itinerary around them.
  - *Reach out.* Email incubators and accelerators to ask if you can network with their companies. These are fledgling businesses that often will be happy to talk to someone with any sort of relevant expertise.
  - *Be vocal.* Tell your coworkers and friends what you're interested in and where you're going. Announce what

you're looking for on social media. Ask for recommen-
dations on whom to meet and where.

○ *Use what you have.* Offer up your own skills, whether
for a short consultation or a longer period, in exchange
for being able to speak to and shadow people at the
company. Exchange knowledge and network while you
do it.

The Man Who Knew a Lot

*"You know how funerals are not for the dead, they're for the
living? Bachelor parties are not for the groom, they're for
the uncommitted."*

—BILL MURRAY

It's 2014 at a steakhouse in Charleston, South Carolina.
A group of drunk friends are celebrating the soon-to-be
groom among them. They're young and happy and a little basic. Slide your gaze across the room to another table,
which for dramatic effect is in a dark corner of the otherwise well lit space. Bill Murray looks up from a fruity cocktail. His face is lined with equal parts misery and mischief.
He catches sight of the rowdy crew. Expression unreadable,
he picks up his drink and saunters over to their table. As
soon as he starts talking, the crowd hushes (except for the
occasional good-natured laugh), because he's much more
famous than they are.

(Please excuse these entirely fabricated details; the quotes, and the gist—that Bill Murray crashed a bachelor party—are 100% true.)

He says, "If you have someone that you think is the one, don't just sort of think in your ordinary mind, 'OK, let's make a date, let's plan this and make a party, get married.' Take that person and travel around the world. Buy a plane ticket for the two of you to travel all around the world. And go to places that are hard to go to, and hard to get out of. And when you come back to JFK, when you land at JFK, and you are still in love with that person, get married at the airport."

Facts & Figures: Bill Murray

Born: 1950.

Seasons on *Saturday Night Live*: Three.

Agent: None; he has a 1-800 number you can call with your pitch.

Parties Crashed (Bachelor and Otherwise): Unknown, but a lot.

Bill's right. He's also deeply strange, but he's still right. If you want to test your relationship, or get a feeling for the longevity of a friendship, travel with that person. Travel forces you to face challenges and celebrate joys together with a partner. In days or even hours, you'll learn more about another person than you could in a lifetime of sharing an office or a couch.

Are they organized? (Packing, planning, logistics.) How are they with finances? (Tracking spending, splitting costs, splurging.) What are they like to live with? (Sharing cramped rooms, hogging bathroom supplies, smooshing together on a bus.) How do they handle pressure? (Rushing around, operating in a new place, not speaking the language.) Are they fun? (Tequila shots, museum games, being chased by monkeys.)

Let's do some math: If you see a certain friend one night a week for three hours, in one year you would have spent less time with them than you would on a week-long vacation together. Friendships are built and destroyed on the road. Lifetime connections are found in unexpected places, and bonds you thought unbreakable dissolve under new conditions.

If you love someone, or think you might want to love them, take them on a trip. The best bonds will be strengthened, and the weakest bonds—well, it's probably for the best that you figured this stuff out now, rather than a decade into marriage, right?

Souvenirs:

- Bill Murray told a bachelor party to forget planning a wedding and instead travel.
    - Traveling with someone is the best glimpse into their true character, and the true strength of your bond.
- George Megre and Bill Murray are best friends who travel the world together on a party cloud.
    - False, but would be excellent.
- Bill Murray once started bartending in a random bar. Whatever the patrons asked for, he gave them a shot of tequila. The customers did not mind. He then went to hang out with the Wu Tang Clan.
    - True story.

Getting Around

We've spent a lot of time discussing how the amount of time you spend traveling increases the benefits you'll get. In this vein, I've encouraged you to go deep rather than broad. But let's take a moment to consider the flip side. How many places are you traveling to? What does breadth of travel get you?

It turns out that the more places you go, the more trust you have. Specifically, there's a generalized trust you develop toward people in a society not your own. When things are very foreign, and you're unused to foreign, it can be hard to really believe that everything is going to be okay. But any society only ever functions because we trust that it will. We all maintain a certain level of trust with strangers in our own society, and we have to learn to extend that same trust to strangers elsewhere. If you don't develop that depth of trust, you'll have a hard time really letting go in the way you need to develop real connections and take real risks. And if you don't have even a little of that trust, you won't be able to eat at a foreign restaurant for fear of food poisoning.

In one research paper, Professor Galinsky and his team examined this generalized trust in five different studies of American and Chinese participants, The studies demonstrated that individuals who had been to more countries had higher generalized trust than those who had spent a significant amount of time in fewer foreign countries—i.e., that breadth of travel led to more trust than depth of travel.

What does all that say about networking? Well, those countries you traveled to are full of people. The more people you get to know, the more trust you will have in people in general, and the more possibilities you will open yourself to. Speaking selfishly, I would never have been able to write this book if I didn't have a network full of generous travel enthusiasts. As the old saying goes, "It's not what you know but who you know."

There's also a deeper resonance to the importance of having people in your lives. In an increasingly connected world, it's still easy to feel disconnected. Technology can bring people together, but it also makes you feel more alone when that screen turns off. In fact, by some estimates, as many as 46% of Americans over the age of eighteen have reported "sometimes or always feeling alone." That number is only getting bigger. People with chronic loneliness, the more permanent version of that feeling, are at risk of having a shorter lifespan, higher blood pressure, and faster cognitive decline. So by building relationships, you're not just increasing your chances at success, you're making it more likely you'll live a longer, stronger life.

Of course, knowing more people doesn't always mean you'll feel less lonely. Not all connections are quality connections. Meeting someone at a bar doesn't mean they'll recommend you for a job, or lift you out of a depression. But they *might*. And having significant experiences with people, like you can do while traveling, makes relationships deeper and more lasting. Even if you're not going to an event or taking a trip with someone, just sharing stories about your respective study abroad trips is more likely to bond you than chatting about your favorite car or TV show. So get busy living, and sharing that life with others.

Suggested Itinerary: Building Your Network

- Meeting new people can be awkward, but it's worth doing because you never know when a random acquaintance will turn out to be a life-saver.
    - Use your existing network as a starting point: tell friends, including on social media, about where you're going, and ask for tips and introductions.
- Once you start building that network, keep it up. Reach out, keep in touch, and meet in person whenever possible.
- The best way to get a job, create your own job, or be the best at what you're doing is to have a network that you can leverage.
- If you're truly uncertain of what's best for you, meeting more people and learning what they do makes it more likely that you'll find something right.
    - How do you even know if what you're doing is best for you if you don't know what else is out there?
- Not only can travel help you build a network, it can deepen it too; traveling with friends and loved ones forges bonds like nothing else.

SPIRITUALITY

"Travel isn't always pretty. It isn't always comfortable. Sometimes it hurts, it even breaks your heart. But that's okay. The journey changes you; it should change you. It leaves marks on your memory, on your consciousness, on your heart, and on your body. You take something with you. Hopefully, you leave something good behind."

—ANTHONY BOURDAIN

Roadmap

Spirituality these days is a squishy subject. This book won't ask you to join a monastery or convent, take a vow of silence, or take a three-month pilgrimage around the 88 temples on the island of Shikoku, Japan. (To be clear: you are welcome to do these things, and they may be varying degrees of amazing for you, but it's not the level of practicality we're aiming for in *The Traveler's Edge*.) The version of spirituality we're considering here is focused on becoming more at one with yourself, others, and the world at large. We're talking about realizing that there is more to life than the self, and that there is more to the self than you've probably considered for most of your life.

Our second chapter delved into the ways that travel gives you perspective and makes the world seem like a bigger, more interesting place. Often through this exercise we discover a desire to dedicate our time and energy to causes greater than ourselves. It's no coincidence, then, that altruism and philanthropy are everywhere in this book. Some stories involve people making themselves rich, others demonstrate how people learned to get more out of earning less—but nearly everyone we've talked about has unearthed some version of the desire to accomplish a greater good. (This wasn't always explicit in their stories as set out here because that would be a bit repetitive, but I promise those elements were virtually always there.)

We've already discussed at length why you should enrich yourselves with out-of-the-ordinary experiences. We've talked about improving your material life, your thought processes, and your emotional state. But the next step is to enrich your spirit, your psyche, or whatever you want to call those parts of you that can't be captured in the convenient metaphors of your body, heart, and mind. In this chapter, we will consider how travel has led individuals down a path of spirituality, and how searching for that sort of enlightenment can lead to success (even if it's not the success you were looking for).

Top Sights

Won't You Be My Neighbor?

"The more [Americans] get out of the U.S. to travel, the better the chances are for kinds of things like peace, understanding, and decent inter-governmental relations."

—FRED ROONEY

Fred Rooney's journey began when he was just a kid in Garden City, New York. Fred developed a fascination with what would become his second language after his fourth grade teacher taught the class to count to ten in Spanish. Fast forward to college, when he elected to go abroad for a year to build his proficiency and learn more about Latin American culture. When classmates and teachers told him to go to Spain, Fred bristled. "I wanted to go to Latin America, and people were telling me that I was nuts because back in the early '70s people had no concept of what it was about. But it did really change my life in a meaningful way and set the stage for the rest of my life until now."

So in his junior year, Fred studied abroad in Bogotá. In that time, he became very aware of the country's wealth disparity and how so many were living in poverty. Fred had always been interested in helping other people, but his experiences in Colombia made him determined to do work that would serve those less privileged. This commitment to service would not just be a career for him, but a spiritual calling to go above and beyond to do whatever he could for his fellow humans.

In the decades since that trip, Fred has made good on his goal. According to a friend, Fred's work has saved "hundreds, if not thousands, of people's lives. Literally. He finds money for sick children to get a surgery they can't afford. He represents women who need to leave abusive relationships. He makes sure people have heat in their apartment during the cold New York City winters. He finds scholarships for kids to go to college. He opens his home to strangers. The list goes on and on."

Fred continued to travel after that initial perspective-shifting journey. He lived in Israel and Puerto Rico, and spent significant time in India and Cuba. He was particularly attracted to places that had very specific narratives to the average American, as he quickly learned that his perceptions of these places could not be farther from the reality. Eventually, Fred came back to the U.S. to pursue a career as a social worker and English instructor for immigrants. But he soon changed course again.

"During my years working with immigrants, I was able to see how difficult life is in a foreign country where immigrants are not always welcome. Many of my clients/students were victimized by discrimination and racism. I realized that to be more effective as an advocate for the most marginalized and vulnerable members of my community, I needed to become a lawyer."

But being a lawyer wasn't a magic bullet; like many lawyers, Fred realized, "Law school doesn't teach you how to practice law." Instead, most recent grads depend on mentors and employers to guide them through the practicalities of the legal system. For JDs with jobs at law firms or well known service organizations, this was no issue. But Fred wanted to strike out on his own, to do the kind of legal work that he knew was necessary from his own experiences abroad and doing social work. And Fred wanted to help as many people as possible rather than simply chase the dollar.

After all, Fred follows the creed of Stephen Grellet, a Quaker missionary: "I expect to pass through this world but once; any good thing therefore that I can do or any kindness I can show to any fellow creature, let me do it now. Let me not defer or neglect it for I shall not pass this way again."

So he put in the work to figure out how to blaze his own trail, and that trail led him right back to law school. Fred wanted to help other young lawyers avoid the pitfalls that he faced during his early years. He created a legal incubator system at the law-school level, modeling his organization after incubators in other industries (tech, graphic design, even baking). He provided a way for new lawyers to get the mentorship that his legal education didn't want to provide. There are now over 60 of these incubators around the U.S. And through all of them, there is the core principle that Fred learned, to hone your skills by helping those in need.

"When I was young, I always believed that I could change the world. As I got older, I realized that changing the world wasn't a realistic goal, but helping to change the lives of individuals so that their lives were more rewarding and fruitful was a more achievable goal. Once I became a lawyer, I quickly found out that lawyers can be catalysts for social change, brokers for justice and equality and valuable members of society when they use their knowledge and skills to ensure the rights of each individual in our community are respected and protected."

Fred has been doing this work for decades, and has begun to expand his vision internationally. "Through my travels, I would interact with lawyers from all over the world, and everyone would tell me the same thing, that everybody had the same issues when it comes to the legal system." His incubators have now expanded to the Dominican Republic, Spain, and Pakistan.

Fred is also both a Fulbright Scholar and a Fulbright Specialist, meaning he is part of a cultural exchange program seeking to improve intercultural relations, cultural diplomacy, and intercultural competence between the U.S. and other countries through the exchange of persons, knowledge, and skills.

The difference between a job and a calling is simple: you do a job as a means to an end (to put a roof over your head, to provide for your loved ones, etc.), but a calling is an end in itself. What transforms a job into a calling is the spiritual clarity that Fred found in Bogotá and keeps finding in his work today.

Most lawyers don't love their jobs, but Fred does. "As lawyers, we have the potential to engage in the ongoing creation of a world that truly strives to embrace the notion that all men and women are created equal and therefore deserve to be treated as such. Helping to improve the lives of the most vulnerable members of our community, while also ensuring that we are able to adequately support ourselves and our families, will make the practice of law more analogous to a vocation than to a profession and will inevitably make that world a better place in which to live."

Souvenirs:

- Fred Rooney is inspired by the ways that real people, especially people from different countries and cultures, can defy the preconceived notions we have of each other.
  - It's easy to have wrong-headed ideas about people who are different from you if you never bother to get to know them. But we all owe it to each other to treat each other as people, first and foremost. Start there, rather than with assumptions, and you'll find a lot of common ground.
- Fred's travels initially led him to do social work; he later pursued a law degree in order to establish himself in the position from which he could do the most good.
  - Once you've figured out your inspiration, assess what qualifications you need to have the greatest impact. Sometimes, a few more years of school are worth the effort—especially when they will help you help more people.
- Fred saw the shortfalls in his legal training and sought to solve that problem for others, all while continuing to promote his priorities of serving those in need.

- If you're passionate about your work, if you consider it a calling rather than a job, you will want to share it with everyone.

From Middle America to Latin America

"The problem [is] when you have a piece of bad news and a piece of good news, you go to the bad news first because your brain is psychologically wired to. It's a fight-or-flight kind of thing and you are trying to survive. … I think that we can reprogram the psyche of the world to see the hope and the good and love before we see the despair and the hate and the misery."

—BRIAN RASHID

Brian Rashid is one of the top branding and messaging experts in the world. His company, Brian Rashid Global, helps companies and individuals share their stories and grow. He regularly contributes to publications such as *Forbes, Entrepreneur,* and *The Huffington Post.* Before starting his own business, Brian was a speechwriter for Mike Bloomberg's administration when he served as Mayor of New York. And before all of this, Brian was just a kid from the Midwest who had never left the country. Mostly, his life was football. Brian loves his hometown and he looks back fondly at his time in the Midwest, but he does admit that it could be described as insulated, a place where he "wasn't exposed to much global thinking or global curiosity." But then, those football skills got him a scholarship to Butler University in Indiana.

Two years and too many concussions later, Brian hung up his helmet. For many young athletes, this would sound like the end. But for Brian, it was "the best thing to ever happen" to him. Without the pressures of football, he started doing things like spending more time with his friends. Those friendships would lead him to visit Berkeley, California, and his first taste of life outside his middle-America bubble. It was a culture shock, but he found himself feeling more at home in the eccentricities of San Francisco than he had been in the Midwest. With the help and encouragement of his friends and teachers, Brian decided to move to San Francisco. He was the second person he knew from his hometown that made it out of the Midwest. From San Francisco, he jumped to the other coast, to law school at the City University of New York ("CUNY").

At CUNY, Brian was introduced to none other than Fred Rooney, who was developing his first legal incubator. Brian had already been considering spending a summer somewhere he could learn Spanish, and Fred connected Brian to an orphanage in the Dominican Republic where he could help underprivileged children.

During his summer in the Dominican Republic, Brian did a lot more than help and brush up on his Spanish. Shortly after his arrival, Brian discovered that the orphanage's 125 children were regularly getting sick because of fumes from garbage being burned at the dump just behind the building. Brian wasn't having it. He helped rally the community, politicians, and the media around helping the orphans, even if it meant inconveniencing their trash habits.

Brian received an unexpected show of gratitude for his efforts. "It was a very, very powerful experience. In the last night at that orphanage, every single one of the kids gave me a gift. Every single one of these kids, who had the worst stories you could imagine, gave me a gift—a bracelet, a necklace, a love letter, a hug or something. And I remember I was there with a woman named Marcella and I told her, 'This is it, I'm dedicating my whole life to Latin America.'" Brian had caught the same bug that Fred did. In fact, he spent the next summer in Buenos Aires, working in public health and nurturing his love for service.

Brian still goes back to the orphanage even now, a decade later. It gives him a sense of fulfillment to see that his work has made a definitive impact on the quality of life for all the children that live there. His soul is nourished by watching them enjoy playing outdoors and get to be regular kids. It's also a reminder of how he found his life's purpose: not just the abstract of philanthropic work, but the specific task of helping people by sending a clear message and rallying a community for a cause. Today, Brian's work isn't all charity, but it is all about sending a message—though he does keep up his *pro bono* work as well.

Like Fred, Brian is a Fulbright Specialist. His project seeks to empower orphans in the Dominican Republic with the digital tools they need to succeed in modern-day business. He also runs an entrepreneurship competition called "Uniting the Americas." The competition chooses two entrepreneurs, one from North America and one from Latin America, to receive Brian's mentorship, a trip to Silicon Valley, and $10,000 of seed funding. The winners met with senior executives at major tech companies, connected with venture capitalists to pitch their ideas, and grow their ideas to their full potential. The next round of the competition will also be made into a documentary to show how these amazing entrepreneurs are doing good for the world.

"The thing that I took away [from my travels] was that people are inherently generous in their heart. What always surprises me is how quickly people are willing to open up their homes"—even to foreigners like him. So he's found a way to open himself to others as well, and to encourage the rest of the world to do the same. And he finds all of the work fulfilling, now that it centers on his talent and passion of communicating with people, finding the best medium to spread a message, and using those connections to help people accomplish things they could not do alone.

Souvenirs:

- Brian Rashid grew up in a small town in Illinois and never met people really different from him until he was in college.
  - Don't wait for the world to come to you; the sooner you get outside your bubble, the more time you'll have to find yourself and your passions.
- Brian's quest to learn Spanish morphed into a spiritual awakening. He has centered his career on his love for connecting people and ideas, with plenty of time for pro bono work focusing on Latin America.
  - We've talked about the idea of a calling in the context of service, but work doesn't have to be purely philanthropic to be a vocation. Charity work can be just a part of the mosaic of what you love to do.

The Long and Winding Road

"In the end, you're trying to find God. That's the result of not being satisfied. And it doesn't matter how much money, or property, or whatever you've got, unless you're happy in your heart, then that's it. And unfortunately, you can never gain

perfect happiness unless you've got that state of consciousness that enables that."

—GEORGE HARRISON

Everyone knows the story of four boys from Liverpool who changed the world through a combination of experimental pop music and mop-top haircuts. And everyone knows that John Lennon and Paul McCartney were the main composers for The Beatles. But true Beatles fans also appreciate the many incredible contributions of the third Beatle, a.k.a. anyone but Ringo Starr.

George Harrison has long been known as "the quiet Beatle." He didn't seem to have a problem with that moniker, instead proclaiming, "I wanted to be successful, not famous." But even without the pressure of being a front man, stardom got old. At one point, George and his fellow Beatles grew sick of touring; the fans were screaming so loud that they could barely hear the music. So in 1966, they called it quits. George famously said "Right—that's it, I'm not a Beatle anymore!"

However, that wasn't the end. George and his band mates would, of course, return to The Beatles, but not without a significant detour. After years of performing for others, George took the time to look within for spirituality. He grew interested in Eastern philosophy and began experimenting with playing Eastern musical instruments. (You can hear and see the results on *Sgt. Pepper's Lonely Hearts Club Band*; that's George on the sitar on the song "Within You, Without You.") George also began practicing meditation, and the other Beatles soon followed suit.

All four ended up doing a spiritual retreat in northern India. That time, and the period following, was their most productive in an outrageously productive musical career. The band wrote more than half the songs for the *White Album* during that retreat, and even Ringo wrote his first song for a solo album. And George was the most affected of all of them.

The change in George wasn't just a creative invigoration, but a new awareness of life, poverty, and suffering. He later said, "I remember thinking I just want more. This isn't it. Fame is not the goal. Money is not the goal. To be able to know how to get peace of mind, how to be happy, is something you don't just stumble across. You've got to search for it." George organized the Concert for Bangladesh in 1971, the first charity concert of the modern era, which went on to inspire more concerts like it in the decades to come.

When The Beatles ultimately called it quits for good in 1970, George had already found his peace. "Down through the ages, there has always been the spiritual path. It's been passed on—it always will be—and if anybody ever wants it in any age, it's always there."

Souvenirs:

- George Harrison and his fellow Beatles quit making music until a meditation retreat in northern Indian rekindled their spirits and sparked some of their best work.
  - Everyone, even the best musicians of all time, gets burnt out. Exploring other cultures, and especially their spiritual practices, can rekindle that flame.
- George's music was inspired, but so was his soul. He continued to be involved and invested in religion, as well as helping those in need, long after The Beatles officially called it quits.
  - Your spirituality will stay with you when everything else (your career, your friend group, your pastel suits) has gone.

Getting Around

By its very nature, finding spirituality is never going to be guaranteed—but that doesn't mean it's not worth chasing. Steve Jobs learned this lesson the hard way.

In the mid '70s, Steve Jobs was a hippy and a college dropout. After saving up some money, he and his friend Dan Kottke went to northern India in search of enlightenment. Perhaps because they were expecting an easy solution and did not actually prepare for the realities of the world outside their

American bubble, they instead found lice, dysentery, scabies, and robbery. Dan later recalled, "I remember us praying to any god that could hear us, 'Dear God, if I ever get through this, I'll be a good person, I promise.'"

Steve eventually saw the error of his initial mindset, recognizing, "We weren't going to find a place where we could go for a month to be enlightened." Spirituality is not a revelation that comes on command, and there is no keyboard shortcut for nirvana.

But something valuable still came out of the attempt. Steve came back to America with a new sense of self-awareness and drive. He ended up founding Apple shortly after his return, and Dan became one of Apple's first employees just after that. Steve was so convinced of the transformative utility of his travels that he directed Mark Zuckerberg to try the same. Mark then spent a month in India reminding himself of the value of connection. "[H]aving the opportunity to feel how much better the world could be if everyone had a stronger ability to connect reinforced for me the importance of what we were doing. And that is something that I've always remembered over the last ten years as we've built Facebook."

Spiritual enlightenment is a lofty goal, and there's no guarantee you'll ever make it, but trying will still get you somewhere good. And if you travel without expectation and with an open heart, you may just stumble upon more than you bargained for. That's what happened to Fred and Brian, whose travels inspired them to transform their jobs into the vocation of helping others. Because of their deep connection with what they do, both men have no doubt that they would continue their work even if it didn't make them money. In fact, both are now successful enough that much or all of the work they do is *pro bono*.

Spirituality can give you purpose regardless of who you are or where you are in life. Fred builds legal incubators as a full-time job; Brian continues helping the Latin American community through his many side projects; and George used his fame to raise money and bring attention to important causes while pursuing his inner peace.

You can turn your calling into a job, you can use your job to support what matters to you, or you can keep what nourishes your soul and what pays your bills totally separate. These are all valid choices that you can make once you get in touch with that deeper level of meaning. Otherwise, you'll never know what kind of fulfillment you're missing out on.

Suggested Itinerary: Deepening Your Spirituality

- There is no one meaning of spirituality: it's whatever you think there is beyond your body, heart, and mind. However, that uncertainty makes it all the more worthwhile to pursue.
- You can't go traveling expecting spiritual enlightenment, but if you keep your heart open, you might be surprised by what you learn about the world and yourself.
- If you find a cause you believe in wholeheartedly, you can transform your life—by moving, by switching careers, by getting another degree, etc.—to pursue your calling.
    - That said, your passion *doesn't have to* be your whole life. It can be just as rewarding to pursue these things in your free time, or as a side hustle.
- Spirituality can reinvigorate your work, and it can stay with you long after your work is done.

PART 3

MEANS OF TRAVEL

DESTINATION 8

STUDY

"Out there things can happen, and frequently do,
To people as brainy and footsy as you.
And when things start to happen, don't worry, don't stew.
Just go right along, you'll start happening too!"

—DR. SEUSS, *OH, THE PLACES YOU'LL GO!*

Roadmap

It's never too late to travel, but the earlier you do it, and the more you do it, the better. If you're fortunate enough to be reading this as a young whippersnapper, you have the unique opportunity to distinguish yourself from your peers by being the worldliest student on the block. This chapter will discuss your best options to combine your travel education with your academic education, whether by taking a gap year or by studying abroad. We'll look at how statistics, personal experience, and academic expertise all add up to the same message:

Study abroad.

If you're currently in the job market or even just exploring career listings, you may have noticed that many companies are pushing for candidates who have had international exposure. Job postings often have sections called "Competencies" or "Qualifications" with requirements like "international mindset" or "adaptability and willingness to work with people from different cultures." As every industry becomes more global, companies are recognizing the need for employees with experience working in foreign environments; even if it's not technically a prerequisite, this kind of experience will give you a leg up.

Similarly, universities and other institutions have long recognized the value of international experience, providing opportunities for ambitious students to get that exposure. Most colleges have an option for students to do a semester, year, or summer abroad. Some masters programs are even *requiring* some foreign experience to graduate. For example, many top-tier business schools require their students work on an international project and present their findings to their assigned companies abroad:

- Columbia has a Global Immersion Program that requires MBA and EMBA (Executive Masters in Business Administration, catered toward people with full-time jobs) students to work on a semester-long project with an international company culminating in an onsite visit.
- Georgetown's business school has a mandatory Global Business Experience that does the same, but also intentionally times the travel to coincide with spring break. The school encourages its MBAs to use their time off to travel further and immerse themselves in new cultures.
- Harvard Business School has a similar mandatory program for first-year students called FIELD (Field Immersion Experiences for Leadership Development). Harvard builds on this requirement by offering multiple second-year electives in which students continue to apply their learning by traveling to multiple countries around the globe.

All of these programs are offered in addition to the normal semester-long study exchanges with other institutions around the world. In short, these opportunities are so valuable that they are multiplying, and rapidly transforming from opportunities to requirements. The choice is clear: get ahead of the travel learning curve, or fall behind.

Top Sights

Presidential Seal of Approval

"We have a responsibility as a liberal arts school to expose students to things that may make them uncomfortable—but that is a part of our world, a part of our society. If we don't expose them to that, then we're not doing our job."

—BRYON GRIGSBY

Bryon Grigsby is the President of Moravian College, a private liberal-arts school in Bethlehem, Pennsylvania. Moravian has a rather fantastic study-abroad statistic: 23% of their students study abroad, more than twice the national average of 10%. But according to Bryon, that figure isn't good enough. He wants to have 100% participation.

"There isn't an industry that you can come up with that isn't globally connected … every single industry right now is a global industry, so not having those experiences and being able to navigate difference will put you at a disadvantage," says Bryon.

> **Facts & Figures: Moravian College**
>
> Founded: 1742.
>
> Undergraduates: About 1,700.
>
> Endowment: $102 million.
>
> Notable Firsts: Moravian was the first college to teach women, and the first to teach Native Americans in their own language.

Bryon's goal is to make all of his students global citizens, a lofty aim for a school whose students largely come from middle-class families. The average student at Moravian comes from a family that makes $95,000 a year; compare that to a large private university such as University of Pennsylvania, where the average student's family makes $196,000, and you'll start to get a sense of how high Bryon is aiming. Because Bryon's students are less likely to come from a background of privilege, they are less likely to have had international travel experience.

Unsurprisingly, Bryon says the two largest roadblocks preventing students from going abroad are financial hardship and fear of the unknown. In response, he's made it a priority to have school-sponsored trips with faculty supervision, and offer those trips during times of the year when students can participate without academics, sports, or anything else getting in the way. With this framework, Bryon says, "You took away the fear of finances because the institution funded the trip. And you took away fear [of the unknown] because you go with a trusted faculty member that has lived or studied in that country."

But the school isn't just giving students free tickets to tourist traps. Each of these trips are immersive cultural experiences: "Students would go with a faculty member to, let's say, Jordan. They will spend ten days to two weeks not necessarily being a tourist, but trying to experience that environment openly from a global situation. So you might be visiting water reclamation areas, you might be visiting a college or a high school, you might be visiting a mosque. You'll do some tourist things but for the most part you're there to actually interact with the people who are there."

Bryon's goal is to help students escape the tourist mindset. He says, "If you're going just as a tourist and you're going to tourist locations you're seeing more people like you. … That is markedly different when you are going to a location where you are the other. You are the one that has to navigate, there aren't people taking care of you, you are taking care of yourself. You are having to make friends and make connections and asking for help." Navigating a new place and learning how to ask for help are invaluable life skills for young people to learn, and Bryon is happy to provide these lessons from the institutional standpoint.

Travel also comes with broader cultural lessons. By interacting with new people, Bryon says, "You learn that your one way of doing something or your seasoned way of doing it is not necessarily the right way or wrong way. There are different ways to approach different issues. It makes you more well-rounded, it takes away that concept that different is deficient. No, different is not deficient, different is just different. [But] if you get to evaluate differences, you may choose that your way is not the best way of doing it and now you have a different way of doing it." Bryon is planting the seed of curiosity and self-reflection in Moravian students. Not to mention the simple boon of making his students get passports—a tool that 58% of Americans don't have.

Bryon is convinced that his efforts are having great results. He's seen countless students become enthralled with travel—many go on to do a study-abroad program or join the Peace Corps. And, though it's less easily quantifiable, Bryon believes his more globally apt and aware students have also learned a desire to serve their communities and help their fellow humans.

Souvenirs:

- Even though students of Moravian College are less likely to come from privileged backgrounds, the school has seen incredible participation in study abroad thanks to an institutional program that removes financial impediments and fear.
  - It's important to recognize what's holding you back from travel. These difficulties may be entirely valid, but once you name them, you'll have an easier time finding the specific opportunities that let you work around them, whether that's a scholarship program, mentoring, or something else.
- President Bryon Grigsby makes sure that the school-funded trips are not simple vacations, but immersive, interactive experiences that teach real life skills.
  - College these days is not just about learning advanced math or reading the complete works of Plato; schools want to teach you how to be an open-minded, self-sufficient citizen. Mindful and purposeful travel, like the kind Bryon fosters, can teach you these skills.

Siesta en España

Coming out of college, my biggest regret was not having done a semester abroad. When I decided to go to graduate school, I knew I wanted to get that international experience before returning to the workforce, even though I only had four semesters of business school to look forward to. So I signed up for a semester in Barcelona.

A few weeks before that semester, I was at the tail end of an intensive summer internship as an investment banker. Out of the 70 days of that summer program, I was in the office for 68, working until 2 a.m. or later. Somehow, I kept on keeping on. But just as the light at the end of the tunnel was clearly visible, a boulder was dropped on me: I was not going to get a full-time offer. I was devastated. I was supposed to leave for Barcelona in two weeks, but now panic set in—how could I go abroad when I didn't have a position lined up for after graduation?

My first thought was to pull out from the program so I could focus on securing a job. The only other options were to do a job search while I was on a different continent or, even worse, be on the hunt while in my final semester. But for some reason, I didn't back out. Maybe I was just too burnt out; maybe I wasn't willing to give up on my dream of going abroad; maybe I was just dumb—probably a combination of all three. But regardless, I decided to stick with my plan.

I won't sugarcoat it. Looking for a job in the U.S. while living in Spain was both difficult (the internet and phone service were unreliable, and I couldn't network in person) and frustrating (I ended up coming back in late December still unemployed). However, my time abroad was one of the most memorable and fun periods in my life—and it had the added benefit of helping me go down a different path. After I came back to the U.S., I was more focused than ever during my final semester. I felt reinvigorated. It was my best semester academically. In the end, I landed a buy-side M&A opportunity shortly after graduation. That job was a world of difference from my investment banking experience; it made me energized and excited rather than drained and full of dread.

Souvenirs:

- I missed the chance to study abroad when I was in college, but when the opportunity came again during grad school, I seized it.
    - There is no single right moment to go abroad. Take the chance, whenever it comes around.
- When I didn't get a full-time offer out of my summer internship, I considered canceling my semester abroad in order to focus on my job search. I didn't. Even though it was more work, I also had more fun, and was still able to get a surprisingly good post-grad job in the end.
    - Even if you want to study abroad in theory, the practical effect of what you're leaving behind (friends you'll miss, classes you want to take, internet you want to *work*) can seem daunting. The benefits might not feel as real when you're at home, but I promise they're there!
    - It's not that you're putting real life on hold; it's that you're broadening your notion of what is your real life, and prioritizing your long-term goals.

Pantelis's Labyrinth

"You have to get comfortable with the fact that you're not going to know everything. Once you get comfortable with this fact, that's when things become a whole lot easier."

—PANTELIS COLAKIS

Pantelis Colakis has had more study- and work-abroad experiences than most. Born in Athens, he attended an American high school in Greece, went to university in Boston, worked in finance in New York, got a graduate degree in Copenhagen, and finally returned to New York to work with a company headquartered in San Francisco. His extensive travels have taught him many lessons on the ways that diversity makes for better people and better ideas.

Recalling his varied education, Pantelis believes that Denmark had the best way of teaching. Rather than assign students to work with the same group of people for a semester or project, Copenhagen Business School assigns students to sit and work with a different group every day. That way, you are constantly challenged by different personalities, cultures, and perspectives. Pantelis had long developed an appreciation for diversity, but experiencing it so literally on a daily basis drove home the notion that the best ideas can come from anywhere and everyone. Whereas some schools encourage zero-sum competition where each student struggles against their fellows for a spot at the top, Pantelis's school made him the best version of himself by keeping him humble and willing to learn. In this environment, he was able to move away from the self-centered mindset, learning that the strongest course of action often requires that you admit when you are wrong.

Pantelis now works as one of the business development leads for DrumWave, a data analytics company. The company, based in San Francisco, has employees all over the world, and particularly in São Paulo. Pantelis is glad to have the same diversity available to him that he grew accustomed to during his education. "Working in such a diverse company allows me the opportunity to continue learning regularly. Travel has taught me to be humble and by being humble a whole new world of learning has opened up for me."

Souvenirs

- At Copenhagen Business School, Pantelis Colakis was forced to work with a new group of people every day. He learned the value of humility and openness to others' ideas.
  - Exposure to other viewpoints, especially in an academic setting, makes you stronger by reminding you that others have valuable insights you could not have come to by yourself. As Vanilla Ice said, "Stop, collaborate, and listen."

- Pantelis found a job at a software company with international presence that offers a diversity of people and ideas.
  - Companies are becoming increasingly aware of the good business sense of diversity. If it's important to you (and it should be), find a job that supports this value, so you can continue to grow.

Getting Around

Participation in study abroad programs has been growing consistently in past years. According to UNESCO, the number of students that study abroad has grown by an estimated 12% per year in the 21st century; likely a good portion of this is due to globalization and the growing ease of travel. An annual report released by the Institute of International Education states, "The number of American students studying abroad continues to steadily increase, growing by 2.3 percent in academic year 2016-17 compared to the previous year."

These growth trends make a lot of sense because, according to several surveys, study abroad has proven results both in the classroom and in the workforce:

- 100% of students who studied abroad showed an improvement in GPA afterward.
- 97% of study-abroad participants reported that it helped increase their maturity, and 96% said they had more confidence afterward.

- 90% of students who studied abroad found employment within six months of graduation, and 97% within twelve months. For comparison, only 49% of students who did not study abroad found employment within the year.
- Students who studied abroad averaged 25% higher starting salaries.
- 90% of study-abroad alumni got into their first- or second-choice graduate school.
- 84% of them felt that they built valuable skills for the job market.
- 70% of them claimed that study abroad helped them be more satisfied at work.
- 59% of employers agreed that "study abroad would be valuable in an individual's career later on with their organization."
- On the flip side, almost 40% of companies surveyed said they missed international business opportunities because of a lack of internationally competent personnel.

These are some staggering results. With all that evidence, it is no surprise that higher education institutions are pushing for as much international visibility on your resume as possible. Some career centers even go so far as to have students list international projects they've worked on, or the number of countries that they've visited (yes, vacations included). Aren't you glad you found a legitimate excuse for your spring break in Jamaica?

**

If you can't study abroad—or if you can't get enough of study abroad—there's also the option of taking a gap year before college or graduate school. Gap years, if used correctly (meaning not just a year of staying home and playing video games, unless you're making bank to stream on Twitch) can be a great opportunity. You can get involved in volunteer work, or take on a full-time job or internship to get a head start on your career. At minimum, you'll learn more about yourself, with the added benefit of preemptively avoiding burn-out further down the road.

Once upon a time, gap years were unusual, reserved for people who weren't ready to settle down and go to school. However, people have since realized their value, and some universities are even encouraging them. For example, from the Harvard website: "Harvard College encourages admitted students to defer enrollment for one year to travel, pursue a special project or activity, work, or spend time in another meaningful way." Each year, over a hundred students take them up on this offer. Even Barack Obama's daughter, Malia, took a year off before Harvard to spend time in Bolivia and Peru, where she did extensive homestays to learn Spanish.

Gap years can have many of the benefits of study abroad, with the added boon of more time to immerse yourself in whatever activity interests you. Can't decide on one country? It may be possible to fit in several. Short on cash? Spend part of that gap-year working to save up. Now, you're entering university with international experience *and* work experience under your belt. So many students start college never having taken care of themselves; these people are in for a steep learning curve on life. But students who lived independently during a gap year can go into school prepared to focus on academics, having already mastered (or at least apprenticed in) those basic life skills.

Each year there are 30,000-40,000 "gappers." Studies show that these individuals reap similar rewards to those who study-abroad:

- 98% of gappers reported that their gap year allowed time for reflection and helped them develop as a person.
- 97% of gappers reported an increase their maturity, and 96% in self-confidence.
- 93% reported that gap year helped develop their communication skills.
- 86% said they were satisfied or very satisfied at their jobs.
- 84% acquired skills to help them in their careers.
- 77% found a purpose in their life.
- 75% said that their gap year helped them get a job, and 73% said it increased their readiness for college.

- 72% were inspired to be active volunteers in the global community, and 69% said the same of the local community.
- 63% voted in the 2014 election—compare that to only 18% of their peers.
- 57% reported that their gap year helped them determine what they wanted to study in college.
- 55% had a GPA of 3.7 or above (out of a scale of 4.0), 83% had a 3.0 or above.

In short, the results speak for themselves. So what are you waiting for? You don't need a hall pass. Away you go!

Suggested Itinerary: Making the Most of Study Travel

- You should take a gap year before college or graduate school.
  - You'll learn valuable life skills and can get a jump-start on your interests and/or career goals.
  - If money is an issue, spend the first part of the year working, so you can devote the second part to traveling.
  - There are a lot of structured programs out there for gap years, offering amenities like host families and set curriculums.
- You should study abroad during school.
  - Students who studied abroad get better grades and better jobs.

- Most colleges and graduate programs have a lot of study-abroad options, or in some cases requirements.
- If you're worried about the finances, or you're just plain scared, there are scholarship opportunities and chaperoned trips available too.
- School is not just for learning facts; it's for learning how to live, what other people are like, and what you want out of your future. The more information you get, the better. Travel isn't just the answer; it's also the source of all your best questions.

WORK

"The Jack Welch of the future cannot be like me. I spent my entire career in the United States. The next head of General Electric will be somebody who spent time in Bombay, in Hong Kong, in Buenos Aires. We have to send our best and brightest overseas and make sure they have the training that will allow them to be the global leaders who will make GE flourish in the future."

—JACK WELCH

Roadmap

Business travel is huge and getting bigger. According to the Global Business Travel Association, global business travel spending reached $1.3 trillion in 2017, which was 5.8% more than 2016; that number is expected to increase to $1.7 trillion by 2022.

Also, the travel industry is increasingly catering toward business travelers. For example, Singapore Airlines has recently started flying the longest flight in the world: 19 hours from Singapore to New York City. The flight will only have business and premium economy seating (i.e., no first-class or regular economy), so business passengers are really the focus. The tech world has taken notice, too: Paul English (one of the founders of Kayak) has created a new travel management app, Lola, specifically geared toward business travelers. Unlike what is currently on the market, Lola is easy to implement, more transparent, and very user friendly.

What does all this mean? Well, if you don't already travel for work, there's a good chance you will be asked to do so down the line. If you already do, get ready for some more.

But what if your job is one of the many that doesn't require you to do any travel at all? Well, there are a lot of ways to incorporate travel into your work, or get away with traveling outside of it. What if you want to go beyond the work trips that only scratch the surface of a new culture and environment that you are craving? As we've already learned, business travel can be tedious, but the right attitude can turn it into a unique opportunity to grow ourselves, our network, and expertise.

In this chapter, we will explore all the ways that travel and work can go hand in hand: how you can make the world your office, how you can balance professional and personal goals, and the benefits of becoming an expat at any age.

Top Sights

Permanent Out of Office

"As long as I'm producing, then it doesn't really matter where I am."

—JASON GERSHENSON

Jason Gershenson is a corporate intellectual property and securities lawyer. Most of us know that the legal field requires attorneys to spend countless hours at a desk looking through people's digital footprints. While Jason does plenty of the latter, he's managed to skip out entirely on the "at a desk" aspect of the job. Unlike his coworkers, he is almost never in his company's home office in Portland, Oregon. Instead, you're more likely to find him at home in New York City, colonizing a corner of a WeWork space, or making the job look easy from a coffee shop somewhere else in the wide world.

Jason ended up in this unorthodox arrangement by avoiding the orthodox route. He did not join a big firm straight out of law school and politely declined being chained to a desk. Instead, he specifically carved out a practice area and legal field that granted him this flexibility. First, he says, "I chose a field that's all transactional. I don't go to court; I don't have to meet in person for anything official... Most of the clients that I work with are tech company CEOs, so they're busy, which is good because they don't really want to meet in person." In fact, he has some clients he's never even met in person.

Jason graduated from law school in Oregon, and knew he would spend some time practicing in Portland before returning to his home on the east coast. To accommodate that goal, he made regular trips back to New York, so he could build up his rolodex of clients through legal conferences and referrals. Once he had his own list of clients, he decided to join an established law firm. "There are a lot of skills that I knew I needed to develop by having more experienced colleagues working with me. I could have gone on working solo but I don't think I would have developed as quickly." And although he could benefit a lot from joining a firm, Jason was aware that he brought more value to a firm as an established practitioner than a typical associate; accordingly, he was able to look for an employer who was open to having him work remotely as he preferred.

In short, Jason has carved out a legal career that still allows him the personal freedom to travel at his will. He recently spent a few weeks in Israel, and regularly spends extended periods in Asia. Of course, there are challenges that come with working remotely: calls at inconvenient hours, urgent emails in the middle of the night, and the perennial terror of spotty internet. But Jason has set clear expectations about his timing and availability, and his clients have learned to value his reliability and quality over the immediacy that has otherwise become increasingly important, and destructive, in the legal profession.

Jason believes that, with enough planning and foresight, you can work remotely in any service industry. If a lawyer can do it, why can't you?

Souvenirs:

- Jason Gershenson is a lawyer whose office is in Oregon. He works almost entirely on the road for personal travel or from his home state, New York.
  - If you've developed a desirable skill set or have an established rolodex of clients, then you can negotiate a remote-work strategy with a potential employer.
- Jason is able to avoid the typical lawyer problem of being expected to be constantly on call; part of this was his choice to go into a certain practice area, but part of it is setting clear expectations and delivering on promises.

- Being present and available at all times increasingly feels like a requirement for some jobs, but often at the cost of quality of work and sanity of workers. Consider whether there are ways that you can work around the need for constant availability, and try to establish reasonable guidelines that will benefit everyone.

The Travel Consultant

"I've always loved being a vagabond, but I also wanted the typical career. Who says you can't have both?"

—LILLIAN

Lillian is a consultant at Boston Consulting Group ("BCG"), one of the most prestigious consulting firms in the world. She is also the biggest travel addict you're likely to meet. She chose a career that has her on the move constantly, and she even specializes in working with travel companies (airlines, hotels, cruises, etc.) within consulting. She has been to over 120 countries. She's lived on all the continents except Antarctica (she had trouble finding a penguin roommate that didn't reek of fish). Lillian just got back from a seven-month tour to 28 countries after graduating from Wharton. Oh, and she only recently turned 30.

Although both Lillian and I call the U.S. home, we never actually saw each other on American soil until *years* into our friendship. We first met in Europe, and then traveled together in Asia and Australia on multiple occasions.

Lillian loves her job, her company, and the people that she works with. Over the course of her career, she has had the opportunity to work on projects all over the U.S., Latin America, Europe, and the Middle East. "Out of all the consultants that I know, I've actually had the most control over the subject and topic I work in." Lillian considers herself lucky to work in her preferred area of travel and hospitality, since most young consultants don't get much input on their projects.

In the six years since Lillian was hired at BCG, she's only actually worked for three of them. She spent two of those years at business school, and one just traveling. If Lillian had taken a more conventional path, she'd probably be a partner at her previous consulting firm by now. She made the choices she made because she values life experiences as much as professional progression.

If your goal is to make it up the corporate ladder as quickly as possible, Lillian's model is probably not for you. But Lillian doesn't consider any of her time wasted. As much as she loves her job, she has never treated it as the only focus of her life. Instead of honing in on work to the exclusion of her personal interests, Lillian acknowledges that her personal ambitions are just as important to her as her professional ones. But no one who works with Lillian thinks of her as a slacker; she's undeniably accomplished for her age when you consider her life as a whole, rather than the hypothetical yardstick of how much she would be making if she had never taken a vacation in her life.

Lillian's back at work now in a European office of BCG. And don't worry: she's still got plenty of time for trips.

Souvenirs:

- Lillian, a consultant at BCG, chose a career path that would allow her to travel frequently; but she also took significant time off to focus on personal travel.
  - It's great to find a job that caters to your personal interests, but at the end of the day, it's still a job.
- Lillian accepts the fact that taking time off means she's not as far along in her career as she would be otherwise, because there are more important experiences she's had as a result of her choices.
  - Professional ambition and accomplishments are not the only ambitions and accomplishments that matter; it's okay to fall a little short of the perfect career trajectory if you're able to use that time to do what's important to you personally.

Never Too Old to Be Bold

"No, you are not too old to go abroad."

—KALIL NICOLAS

As a part of Citi's Global Engagement Management Associate program, Kalil Nicolas lived in Shanghai working in cross-border acquisition financing and in Hong Kong working on equity and debt strategic risk solutions. The Citi program is two year-long rotations, followed by a permanent placement based on your career interests, your skill set, and the bank's needs. In Kalil's case, he ended up working in London doing corporate and investment banking.

Basically, Kalil has had the enviable position of traveling around the world working in a number of high-profile business roles for years. Although he thoroughly enjoyed his experience in the program and gained valuable skills, Kalil pointed out that not enough people are taking advantage of the benefits of going abroad midway through their careers.

Kalil calls to attention that in a globalized economy, living and working abroad has unexpected advantages later in your career. Global corporations need well rounded, experienced employees with a global footprint. Larger organizations also value employees that have built a global network across the firm.

In terms of compensation, some companies offer expatriate packages that also make the economics of going abroad very attractive. For example, many companies pay for your housing, your children's education, and other expenditures that would normally take the largest chunk of your paycheck when living domestically. There could also be significant tax benefits--you may be exempt from paying U.S. income tax (up to a point), and your country of work may have more advantageous tax schemes (looking at you, United Arab Emirates).

Kalil points out that there are some short-term sacrifices required to get international experiences. Teams that are highly specialized in a product or industry may not give as much value to such an experience. Similarly, an employee looking to rise through the ranks within a specialized team may see this as a distraction rather than an opportunity. In his view, even if it delays your promotion for one or two years, it will ultimately pay dividends later in your career.

I would add that working abroad has extensive benefits at any point in your career. If your company has foreign offices, they may well consider your transfer, and in some cases compensate you for it. Whenever you make a move to a new roll or a different location it is an opportunity to renegotiate your salary and benefits. Even in instances where you may be relocating from a country with a high standard of living to a lower one it is not uncommon to receive a raise or other benefits.

If you are making an impact to your organization domestically, think about what you could accomplish in a brand new environment. If your company has any doubts about the transfer, it may not hurt to remind them of the costs of employee turnover—which is among the largest harms to an employers' bottom line. Some studies estimate that every employee departure costs an organization anywhere from six to nine months of salary, as the company must recruit and train a replacement.

Souvenirs:

- Kalil Nicolas is part of a global rotational program with Citi. He loves the benefits he gets working abroad in an advanced stage of his career.
  - There is no wrong time to go abroad for work; each stage of your life can have different benefits for you and your family. Working abroad earlier in your career helps you develop valuable skills; doing so later on can have significant monetary and quality-of-life benefits.

Getting Around

As technology changes the way businesses run, work and travel go increasingly well together. Is cubicle life getting you down? As Jason demonstrated, if you set and fulfill clear expectations, you don't have to resign yourself to life in the office. Currently, about 3.2% of working Americans (who aren't self-employed) work from home at least half of the time. That figure has increased 140% since 2005, and is still growing.

One recent study found that, on average, U.S. office workers wasted over eight hours a week on tasks not related to the job (social media, personal errands, etc.). So why waste even more time commuting to an office to do it? The expectation for you to be in an office is shrinking; with technology, many trained individuals have the ability to do their job anywhere. Given the increase in business travel, in some cases it's more vital that you be able to work remotely.

The benefits of working remotely aren't exclusive to employees: Global Workplace Analytics estimates that each remote employee saves a company $10,000 per year just on real estate. They also found that employees who work from home not only work longer hours than their office counterparts, but are also significantly more productive. (For example, AmEx remote employees were 43% more productive than those that worked in the office.)

**

Even better opportunities await you if you're an employee of a company that is willing to relocate you. In addition to the relocation package and a likely salary increase, many companies provide the following for those willing to expatriate: housing, schooling for children under 18, travel back home, and more. As Kalil described, these benefits can be just as great if not better for those later in their careers.

A simple google search will tell you that there are also potential lifestyle benefits to working abroad. Many countries outside the U.S. provide better work-life balance, meaning you'll have more time to spend with family and on leisure. Also, if you're working abroad as a manager rather than an employee, you won't have to worry about adapting to someone else's working style; you will be the one that sets the tone for how everything is done. International companies specifically value your knowledge and experience accumulated through years of work.

Anecdotal evidence not enough? How about some hard numbers:

- On average, expats earned 25% more than they did at home.
- 52% of expats said that they can save more money than they did at home.
- 57% have more disposable income.
- 53% consider themselves to have an improved work/life balance.

- 52% feel that they have a better quality of life.
- 42% take more vacations than they did at home.
- 39% have experienced an improvement in their physical health.

**

Finally, if you only read this chapter for tips on how to get the most out of your business travel, keep in mind that life is about the journey and not the destination.

Per our friend Vincent Liew, "If you are only thinking about your destination you will often miss the wonders that life has to offer." His advice to business travelers: "For almost any trip, you need to find a way to balance enjoyment with work." Even on very short trips, he always looks for a way to integrate taking in the city that he is in. For example, rather than using a hotel gym, run outside and try to take in the pulse of the city. Another simple tip is to skip eating at the hotel; sure, it's convenient, but food is one of the best ways to take in a new destination.

Let's not neglect Julia's advice on networking: try and connect with friends that you may not have seen in a while, or meet up with friends of friends. Even if you don't have particular locals to meet, try to make it easier on yourself to meet new people: for example, consider staying in a neighborhood that would be fun to explore, rather than sticking to the skyscraper-dominated downtown that dies after 7 p.m.

Moreover, you can often turn a business trip into a mini vacation. Bleisure (business plus leisure) travel now accounts for 10% of all business trips; that's a 20% rise from 2017 alone. Most companies won't mind if you alter your departure or return date for a work trip to accommodate some personal time, as long as you're not spending more company money. Have a lot of Monday meetings? Fly out Friday and have a weekend of fun, plus you'll be better rested for Monday morning. Or extend an end-of-week trip into the next weekend. Either way, you're getting a few days of real vacation with a big discount on travel costs. (You'll probably have to pay for a few days of hotel stay, unless you have friends to crash with, but you've still saved a bundle on flights.)

If you're meeting clients in Dallas but want to catch up with your friends in Austin, see if you can find a one-way flight to the first city and a return from the other; then pay out of pocket for a train or bus between the two. Just make sure the two one-way flights are similar to the cost of a roundtrip. This is a simple enough travel hack, but a lot of people don't use it because they're afraid of what their boss may say. Here's a hint: unless you have a particularly finicky employer, they only care about the bottom line. If you can show that there will be no extra cost to the company, you're golden.

And don't forget to use your frequent flyer and hotel loyalty accounts whenever booking business travel (or forward them along to whoever is doing the booking). There's no reason you shouldn't be accruing those rewards to redeem for personal travel.

Lillian's story points out something important about business travel: at the end of the day, it's still for your job. You can, and should, use some of the tips in this chapter and throughout *The Traveler's Edge* to make business travel more meaningful and fun. But that won't magically transform your week in a conference room by the Charles de Gaulle airport into a Parisian getaway. That's okay! If travel is important to you, and the premise of this book is that it should be, you can find room for it otherwise. Lillian's solution for this was to travel for her job *and* take a ton of time to travel for herself. Think about whether that would work for you.

Suggested Itinerary: Making the Most of Work Travel

- Remote work is the new norm. If you never want to step into an office, there's a job for you out there, especially if you have experience and a client list of your own.
  - Be clear on what you are looking for and what can be expected of you logistically (e.g., what time zone you'll be in to answer emails).

- Your personal ambitions don't have to take a backseat to your professional ones. If you want to take some time away from work to pursue your other interests, you can manage it while still being a rock star. Just don't fall into the trap of comparing yourself to the hypothetical robot that would have stayed chained to a desk until retirement.
- Regardless of your career stage, consider working abroad, especially if you are in a multinational company that can do an internal transfer.
  - Be sure to negotiate your relocation package; don't forget the non-monetary benefits.
  - Choose a destination that either caters to expanding you education or allows you to demonstrate your knowledge.
- Business travel can, and should, have its perks, but it's never going to be the same as traveling for yourself. That's okay! If you're doing it right, you should have time for both.

LEISURE

"As you grow older, you learn a few things. One of them is to actually take the time you've allotted for vacation."

—JOHN BATTELLE

Roadmap

The first few minutes of the Pixar movie *Up* offer a succinct reminder of why you shouldn't put off traveling. (If you haven't seen it, please take a break to do so now; I recommend getting some tissues, too.) There is always a reason to delay that dream vacation. Life offers a million excuses, but we are the ones who choose to use them. So many people want to travel, and even have specific trips in mind. Don't wait until it's too late.

According to a report from Project: Time Off, Americans have an astounding **705 million days of unused vacation time** each year. Until recently, the trend had been getting worse: in the last decades of the 19th century, the average American took more than twenty vacation days per year; since 2000, that number has been decreasing, only in the last couple of years did the numbers start to shift upward again to an average of seventeen days per year.

These wasted days are not good for you, and they're not even good for business: 78% of bosses stated that vacations improve employee focus and 81% said that it alleviates burn out. Failure to take time off isn't good for the economy, either. Project: Time Off says we're losing about $255 billion as a result of missing out on job creation and instead building up liability on the books. As we've covered throughout this book, taking the time to travel will make you a better person, including when you get yourself back to the office.

But it isn't about just how many of your vacation days that you take off, it's also about how you use them. Of those seventeen days employees took off, they used only an average of eight to travel. There's also a huge gap in both satisfaction and performance between frequent travelers (who use most of their time off to travel) and homebodies (who use little or none of their days for the same), and it looks like travelers are better off in a lot of important ways.

Project: Time Off on Employee Satisfaction

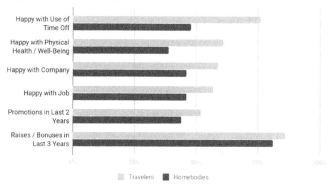

What does all this add up to? Well, despite the constant glorification of a good work ethic, you may actually be hurting your career by working when you should be taking time off, and by using your vacation days to stay home rather than travel.

At this point in *The Traveler's Edge*, you've probably already read a lot of stories of leisure travel, and how to make the most of it. Rather than share more stories about the amazing things people did and learned while traveling for fun, let's focus on more practical tips. In this chapter, we'll talk about the logistics of taking the time to travel for leisure, planning the trip, and who to drag along with you.

Top Sights

Finding Time and Money

Most working Americans start off with an average of ten paid days off, though this number tends to grow as you spend more time with the company. If you're negotiating the terms of a new job, vacation days should be considered right alongside your salary. Is the company a little short of your requested salary, but refusing to budge? Try asking them to increase your paid time off. Some companies will also allow you to take extended unpaid leave; obviously, this isn't a good idea for everyone, but keep the option in the back of your mind in case you wake up one day with a gnawing need to learn to speak Afrikaans or climb Mt. Everest.

Many people spend their vacation days on long weekends or short domestic jaunts. Obviously, there are times and places for these kinds of trips (e.g., that period in your life where everyone you know is getting married and you have to pretend to be excited to go to Phoenix). But, as we've discussed, immersion is often the most effective way to refresh yourself and learn new things. So if you have ten vacation days, consider saving six of them for one long trip. Even allowing for a day or two of travel, this will leave you with over a week to enjoy yourself. You can use the remaining four vacation days to create long weekends, or spend them during an existing long weekend or holiday (if you don't mind a bit of a headache traveling on Memorial Day or Thanksgiving, when everyone else is) for another full week away.

What about the cost? It's so expensive to go overseas these days! You might be pleasantly surprised to learn that that's not always true anymore. If you live in or near a major city or travel hub—which, increasingly, most Americans do—it is often as inexpensive to go to a major destination abroad as it would be to visit a smaller city in America. If you're planning ahead, you can find flights to international capitals at shockingly low prices. There are also online tools (like Kayak's Explore feature) that show you all the destinations that fit your budget and timing; when you're gearing up to spend $500 to go to Orlando, consider taking a look at where else that money could take you.

Keep in mind that the average cost of living can be significantly lower in many places outside of the United States. If you're willing to shell out a little more to get there, you'll spend a lot less on accommodations, food, and entertainment in these places (if you ever paid $12 for a beer in Manhattan, or $0.50 for the same in Prague, you get this). Don't believe it? Do the math. You'll be surprised how often four days in Vegas ends up more expensive than two weeks in Mexico.

Souvenirs:

- Paid time off is a valuable resource you should be considering and negotiating right alongside your salary and other benefits.
- Maximize your access to the magic of cultural immersion by saving at least six of your annual vacation days for one longer trip.
- Travel among major cities is often as inexpensive as flying to a smaller city or town, and you can make up some extra bucks by going somewhere with a lower cost of living. Do the math before you resign yourself to another mediocre trip!

Planning (and Not Planning)

In general, there are two kinds of trips:

- The kind you know you want to do in advance, and
- The kind you won't know about until it's about to happen.

The first kind is the one you plan your year around, saving up your vacation days and coordinating everything. The second, you cannot plan for by definition. Sometimes, you'll see a crazy last-minute deal on a trip to Puerto Rico. Other times, an opportunity will present itself out of the blue thanks to adventurous friends. (If this doesn't sound like you yet, hopefully this book will help nudge you in that direction. Set up some flight alerts, join some deal newsletters, and make more wild friends.)

Assuming you have at least ten paid vacation days, one simple way to make room for both of these types of trips is to put your pre-planned trip in the first half of the year, and save your remaining vacation days for the last quarter. That way, you'll have flexibility if you see an amazing round-trip flight to Tanzania in September. Worst-case scenario, nothing exciting comes up and you take an extra week of time with family or friends around the holidays. (Or convince your friends and family to go somewhere more interesting with you!)

Also, don't forget that most jobs will let you carry vacations over to at least the first quarter of the following year. (For those living in California, you never lose your unused vacation days.) If you don't actually want to use up all your vacation days this year, carry them over to next year so you have time for something more elaborate.

The goal of all this planning, as hopefully has been made clear throughout this book, is to get you to a point where you can take life-changing trips. Living abroad, or at least taking extended vacations that allow for true immersion, increases the likelihood that you will have a meaningful time. At the end of the day, these are all shortcuts to try to help you choose mindful and intentional travel (whenever and however that occurs).

So push the envelope! If you've never left the country, take a trip to a neighboring country in the north or south. If you've only visited Europe, make yourself list all the continents out loud, and pick another one.

Souvenirs:

- Try to plan one interesting vacation in the first half of the year.
- Have some options for a trip in the last quarter of the year, but give yourself flexibility in case a better use for your vacation days comes up. Worst-case scenario, you can go somewhere comforting for the holidays, or roll over unused paid time off.
- Sign up for deal alerts for travel to all the far-flung places of your dreams; they may be more accessible than you think.

Taking You with Me

We've talked about how to travel, when, and how. But what about who? Finding the best person or people to travel with is an important question. As with everything, there is no one right answer to this question. The shortest answer is that you should take whoever will help you travel mindfully and intentionally. For our longer answer, let's consider all the options.

All by Myself

I highly encourage everyone to take a trip alone at least once in their life. For many people, a solo trip will mean the largest transformation in yourself. Why? Because you are more open to experiences and people when you are by yourself. The proverbial safety net is removed: either you'll get comfortable with yourself, or you'll get comfortable with some new people (or both). It's also particularly liberating to have no one to answer to while traveling. Of course, you might also struggle more as a result, but those struggles are what lead to growth. Solo travel is growing in popularity, especially among American women and millennials. After all, if you're ready to see the world and find yourself, why wait for someone else?

Plus One … or Two, or Four

Even the most independent among us can appreciate a vacation with our partner, partner in crime, or crime family. We've already discussed the ways in which travel can deepen your bonds, so by all means, take a trip with your friends and loved ones. Traveling with others can be less expensive, and tagging along with people who are more adventurous, or who already know a location better than you, can be a great recipe for breaking out of your shell.

But traveling with others isn't an exact science: a relationship that works when you can go home to your separate spaces might explode when you're sharing a dinky hotel room. The need for patience, communication, and give and take is exaggerated. Give your companions a break, and ask that they do the same for you. If you feel yourself getting a little fed up, remember that you don't actually have to spend every moment together; take a meal, or a day, off from each other to re-center. And if you find a travel partner that gives you minimal grief and instead multiplies your joy, bring them *everywhere*.

Honey, I Flew with the Kids

Should you bring children on your travels? Yes and no. If you're a parent, you probably already have a good sense of what kind of trip is kid-friendly, and what isn't. Going to the Louvre with a five-year-old in tow is very different from (and much more frenetic than) going alone, but it might be worthwhile to see their eyes turn into saucers at the Egyptian exhibit. As much of a logistical headache as you give yourself bringing the kids, that sense of wonder is a priceless benefit. Traveling from an early age instills a curiosity in children that can pay dividends for life. Most of the most avid travelers I know caught the bug when they were young.

Of course, a sleepy baby will likely be more enamored with your hair than the Mona Lisa's smile, so no worries if you'd rather leave the littler ones with friends or relatives back home. It's great to be a parent who finds time to travel for themselves, and it's great to be a parent who opens their children's eyes to the world. "Where'd you go this summer, Janey?" "Everywhere!"

Anyone, and Everyone, Else

Ernest Hemingway said, "Never go on trips with anyone you do not love." I don't quite agree with that: you probably don't love *everyone* in your birdwatching group, but you could still have an excellent time in Costa Rica together. In fact, traveling with an interest group can be a great way to make new friends while guaranteeing time to do what you enjoy.

But do be wary of the flip side: don't attach yourself to someone who has fundamentally different views on how to spend your time. Sometimes, the people you bring (and don't bring) can be the difference between a life-changing experience and a complete disaster.

Souvenirs:

- Try solo travel, at least once.
- Travel with friends who you want to build an even stronger connection with and those who push you to be more adventurous.

- Bring your kids along for the ride! Just like you, they will get a leg up on their peers who don't travel.
- Remember, airlines make you pay extra for excess baggage, so leave the downers at home.

Getting Around

From July 24, 2015, to February 2, 2017, Cassie De Pecol traveled to every single country in the world. She holds the Guinness World Record for "fastest time to visit all sovereign countries." This is not a thing most people aspire to. And that's fine! She's not exactly the poster child for *The Traveler's Edge*, where we're all about taking our time, developing our understanding of the greater world, and getting in-depth insight into other cultures. Yet, Cassie does bring up one very valid point.

In her TED talk, Cassie says, "Whether you've been to five countries or 150, you probably have your own personal unique experience related to each place. We all have our own way of traveling and discovering a culture and it doesn't matter what you see or where you go, what matters is your own experience while you are there. Some people think that only spending a week or an hour in a country doesn't allow you enough time to see it but there is one thing I know to be true: it's that just one brief experience can shape your whole life."

Is it more likely that you will get more out of an experience if you spend more time on it? Yes. But can a life-changing experience come from anywhere, in any period of time? Also yes! You only learn the little intricacies—the surprising norms, the inside jokes, the local rhythms, with time. But one vital thing about travel is that it will always surprise you. And what could be more surprising, and more typical, than learning some great truth about yourself or the world during a layover?

Regardless of how or how long you travel, this chapter should drive home the fact that you should take more time to travel for fun. Even if you change nothing about your travel habits, make yourself travel more. It is good for your personal life, your job, your family and relationships, and basically every aspect of your life.

Suggested Itinerary: Making the Most of Leisure Travel

- Americans don't take all their paid time off. This is a problem you should start remedying with your own vacation days.
- If you're in a position to bargain for more paid time off, do it. Then plan how to spend those days wisely.
  - Since immersive travel tends to have more benefits, try to save up your vacation days to allow yourself trips of a week or longer.

- If international travel is a priority for you, put in the leg work to find good deals on flights to countries with a lower cost of living than your home.
- Travel solo, travel with loved ones, and travel with random people... just try to share travel with people who will bring out the best in you.
- At the end of the day, any amount of travel you do for fun *should be fun*. Plus, you'll never know what will end up being transformative.

DESTINATION 11

AT HOME

"We shall not cease from exploration
And the end of all our exploring
Will be to arrive where we started
And know the place for the first time."

—T.S. ELIOT, "LITTLE GIDDING"

Roadmap

Not everyone has the time or money to go somewhere new and exciting. And, frankly, you shouldn't *have to* spend an unreasonable amount of time and money to get the benefits of travel. If mindful and intentional travel is as magical as I say it is, you should be able to grow from it without leaving the country, state, or even city you're in. On the flip side, I've also talked about how not all travel is really going to change you, so there must be something special about mindfulness and intention that does the trick. Let's test that theory.

Over the course of our journey, we've delved into how traveling with the right mindset can help you with these seven things: creativity, perspective, confidence, new skills, wellness, network, and spirituality. In our last few pages together, we're going to look at how you can get all of these benefits while traveling the shortest possible distance from your couch.

I'll give you a hint: the secret is to treat your own home like a new place.

Top Sights

Creativity

We've talked extensively about how you can spark your creativity by exploring in depth how other cultures live— but there's also a secret shortcut to this. First-hand experience is great, but you can increase your innovation just by having a close relationship with someone from a different culture.

Professor Galinsky and his colleagues examined data from several different experimental studies on intercultural relationships. They found that individuals who have been in intercultural relationships performed better on various different creative measurement tests, such as divergent and convergent thinking tasks. And just as depth of travel is often more effective than breadth, creativity was most influenced by the length of an intercultural relationship than by the number of such relationships.

Another study looked at 2,226 professionals who were employed in the U.S. before repatriating to their home countries (96 of them, to be precise). The participants who kept in frequent contact with their American friends had more workplace innovation and yielded a higher number of entrepreneurs than those that did not.

So what does that mean? The fastest way from here to Estonia might just be befriending an Estonian. Maintaining lasting and deep relationships with people from different cultures will keep your thinking new and exciting. So get out there and make some new foreign friends!

Souvenir:

- Building and maintaining relationships with people from different cultures increases your creativity.

Perspective

The best way to broaden your perspective is to see how others live differently from you, and force yourself to reckon with why they are the way that they are. As with creativity, interacting and building relationships with foreigners is a great way to do that. But another simple way to understand how you fit into the bigger picture is to meet people from different socioeconomic backgrounds, and especially those less fortunate than you.

Many stories on perspective involve stepping into foreign communities to experience for yourself their struggles with basic necessities. But the sad truth of the world today is that there is probably a community within miles of you that has issues like this. (Consider, for example, how long Americans in Flint, Michigan, did not have access to clean water, and how many suffered as a result.) As the wealth disparity in America widens, your opportunities to find perspective get closer. Volunteer to help. There are places near you that could use a hand providing people with food, water, shelter—or even just an ear to listen. Remember how distant these people *aren't*, and consider what that says about your life. Talk to people you wouldn't normally talk to; see how you differ, and see how you are alike. Perspective will follow.

Souvenir:

- Volunteer work in your community can help you see your own world through different eyes.

Confidence

Confidence comes with practice. You might be confident in one respect, but there was probably a point when you weren't, and probably a ton of other things you're less confident about. Even His Royal Airness Michael Jordan didn't make it onto his high school basketball team until his junior year. Theodore Roosevelt once said, "Each time we face our fear, we gain strength, courage, and confidence in the doing." So there's no pill to engorge your self-esteem; there's just the attempt, the result, and the next attempt.

In the context of travel, confidence comes from having the space to practice and experiment separate from an environment that stresses you. So if you're looking for a place to build your confidence, all that matters is that you look for a place with lower stakes. If you're a kid who is too embarrassed to play basketball with the other kids, you can go to the court very early or very late to get some privacy, or you can find another (less intimidating) group to play with until you're ready. The same is true for us grown-ups. If you're anxious about meeting new people at work, get out of the office; try meeting people somewhere different, like a coffee shop. If you want to build confidence, give yourself leeway to fail, and then you can figure out how to succeed instead.

Souvenir:

- To build confidence in any dimension, try a new (but similar) environment to relieve the stress and find your path to facing your fears.

New Skills

There are two main ways to develop new skills: by having a good teacher, and by trial and error.

Lucky for you, there are willing teachers everywhere. If you're enthusiastic about learning, you just have to put in the effort to find the right teacher for you. Sure, it would probably be better to learn to cook French food in Paris, but those Frenchies had to learn it from the Frenchies before them, and they probably handed it down to some hapless non-continentals too. Julia Child is a famous example of this; she learned to cook later in life, and then brought all those French secrets to a generation of American households. Still not authentic enough for you? We live in the age of YouTube; if you won't settle for anyone short of Daniel Boulud, you can watch him cook from the comfort of your own kitchen. You'll have to compensate a little for the loss of the immersive quality of being in France. Make up for it with rigor: challenge yourself to cook every day as if you were there and stale Wonder Bread just wasn't an option.

As for trial and error, you are just as welcome to try and fail at home as you would be elsewhere. The key is planning and follow through. You wouldn't try to climb Kilimanjaro without meticulous research, a strict preparatory regimen, and all the necessary tools. Apply that same fervor to the highest local peak around, give yourself a few miles and a few days instead of thousands and weeks; you'll still acquire expertise, and Kilimanjaro will be waiting whenever you can get there.

Souvenirs:

- Look for teachers with direct experience, whether in your neighborhood or online, to develop the skills you seek.
- Emulate immersive learning experiences on a smaller scale closer to your own home.

Wellness

Ellen DeGeneres once said, "Procrastinate now; don't put it off!" She was joking, but she also wasn't. If you don't have time for a big vacation to reset your brain, or a month-long boot camp to whip your body into shape, take smaller breaks all the time, and if you can tie those breaks to something good for your body or brain, all the better.

Find regular physical and mental practices that center you, and incorporate them into your routine. Many people find themselves happier and less stressed from just ten minutes of meditation every day. If meditation is too quiet, give your brain something fun to chew on: play a game, or find a trivia night. Also, never underestimate the power of exercise. Exercise releases endorphins, reducing your anxiety and prolonging your life. It even helps fight disease. For example people with breast or prostate cancer (two of the most common kinds of cancers) can reduce their risk of death 40% from just walking a mile each day.

So figure out an exercise practice that speaks to you. I love Muay Thai, but there are countless other options. Yoga and tai chi are popular with millions of people. Want to feel like you're in it together with others? Team sports or dancing might be for you. Practices like this will not only make you stronger, but will provide a regular feeling of accomplishment and progress. And if you like whatever practice you've chosen, it won't feel like just another chore on your list, but a mini-vacation you can't wait to start.

Souvenir:

- Find mental and physical practices that you enjoy, and make them part of your routine—a lot of smaller breaks can keep you centered if you can't take a big one.

Network

In the age of social networking, it's actually amazingly old school to try to meet people *where you are*. But it's absolutely worthwhile. Join an amateur sports league, sign of up for a class you're interested in, or go to events in your neighborhood. Can't find something that interests you? Take it to the next level and create something that people would want to join: a book club, an adventurous eaters' group, a dress-your-pet-in-humiliating-clothing society. The limit is your imagination and your skill at putting up posters.

Or just go full random: a techie named Max Hawkins started to feel trapped in his own bubble in San Francisco, so he developed an algorithm that would search Facebook for random public events in his area. He then started going to events as chosen for him by the app. He ended up meeting people and doing things he never would have imagined (e.g. a community-center pancake breakfast, white Russians with real Russians, and a Christmas party with a retired psychologist). His wish came true: his world got bigger, and he was inspired to expand out of San Francisco next. You don't have to go so extreme, but would it hurt to check out that street fair?

The same principles of networking apply when you're doing it in your backyard: be outgoing, be genuine, and keep up relationships. Your world is only as small as you think it is.

Souvenir:

- Build out your local network by joining groups, checking out events, and going to new places in your own neighborhood.

Spirituality

As we've discussed, there's no surefire way to get at spirituality. It takes work, and often the kind of work you're not used to doing. But one overly simplified way to think of spirituality is to try to turn your insides out, and your outsides in.

The first step to finding meaning can be as simple as getting to know yourself. Instead of filling up your solo time with TV and apps, try to pay attention to yourself like you would a friend. There's nothing wrong with consuming culture to relax, but you might be surprised what you find in your own head when you take the time to listen. Once you get comfortable spending time with yourself, you can then consider how you want to direct your energy back outwards. What brings you joy? What makes you feel bigger than you are?

Another way to get in touch with your spirituality is to sincerely reckon with the notion that other people are as important as you are. How do you put this into practice? Take time to show gratitude and care. When was the last time you showed genuine appreciation to a coworker? When was the last time you thought about what another person needed, and how you could help them get it? Spirituality is often entwined with service for a reason: to be part of something greater, you have to be willing to give more than the norm.

Souvenir:

- Make an effort to look inward and outward with new eyes, listen and act with care, and you just might feel more spiritually connected than usual.

Getting Around

If you happen to live in the United States, then it's worth remembering that most of the people you know are, or come from, immigrants. There are areas in every major city where most people don't speak English. I live in New York, where you can easily convince yourself that you're in

China one second, Poland the next, and Mexico around the block. That's not unique to New York anymore, either. It's not even unique to the United States; everyone is moving everywhere else, and in many places you've never had to go far to hear an unfamiliar language or find a sign you can't read. People adapt to where they go, but they also bring their traditions and cultures with them when they form new communities. And cultures mix, creating things that are new even after millennia of recorded history.

You don't have to go far to be somewhere new. If you're living in the city, find the closest countryside, and take it in. If you're in suburbia, you've probably already escaped to the local metropolis more than once. You can drive, or take a bus, or even bike. Go to a new restaurant, or wander through a park. Just get to somewhere where the air feels different, where things move in ways you're not used to.

You don't even have to go anywhere new. Take a different route to work once in a while, even if it's less efficient. Or take the same route, but let your eyes look somewhere else. Look down, look up. Look at buildings and puddles and trees. Look at people's faces.

Have you ever seen the way that tourists look at the same squirrel you've seen everywhere, as if that plain old squirrel were a magical Disney creature? Or have you been that person on vacation who unabashedly takes a photo of a pigeon as if it were a celebrity? Look at the birds in your hometown as if they were as special as they would be if they came from somewhere else. They do come from somewhere else, and so do you.

Everyone is a foreigner somewhere. *Be a foreigner in your own home.*

Suggested Itinerary: Traveling at Home

- Be a foreigner in your own home.
  - ○ Connect with people from other cultures.
  - ○ Help those less fortunate in your community.
  - ○ Do things that stress you in a less stressful environment, so you can get better.
  - ○ Find teachers for whatever you are looking to learn.
  - ○ Figure out mental and physical practices that you'll look forward to.
  - ○ Try new activities, or the same activities with new people, in your area.
  - ○ Spend time on yourself and on others.

JOURNEY'S END

So we've come to the final pages of our adventure together. For me, this has been a wild ride full of countless ups and downs. I've loved, and sometimes hated, the process of getting the information you've read here. I wasn't sure that I would finish, so I want to thank you all for seeing it through to the end with me. In the end, this book has been another amazing journey in my life. If I manage to encourage just a handful of individuals to travel more, then this was time well spent.

So what are some of my last bits of advice? Are there anymore golden nuggets of knowledge that I can impart before we go our separate ways? Any hidden underlying theme that I've been trying to get across that you may have not unearthed? Here we go, rapid-fire, bonus round:

Travel is not a panacea to all of your life's problems. But sometimes it's enough to have new problems.

If you do not let the journey change you on the inside, then all you've done is change your backdrop. That change is temporary. For real change, look inward and be honest with yourself. Ask, "Am I doing the best that I can? What else can I do to make myself grow?"

Travel will provide you new possibilities for growth, happiness and success—but only if you capitalize on those opportunities when they present themselves. So always stay aware, take chances, and be open to change.

If you don't like where you're living and feel like you don't have any friends to make it worthwhile, moving somewhere new will give you the opportunity to start fresh and meet new people. But if the reason you don't have any friends is because you haven't left the house since Bush was president, then moving your hermit's den to a new city won't help.

I grew up listening to many fables from my father. No matter the situation he had some tale or quip to teach a life lesson. There are too many for me to remember them all, but this one has stuck with me my entire life. One day, a poor man begged God to make him wealthy. His life was so bad that he turned to the power of prayer regularly, so every chance that he got he prayed to God, "Lord, please make me rich." Nothing happened, but the man stayed determined in his prayer. "Lord, please make me rich. Please make me rich." Every day, he prayed to God from dusk to dawn. He got so desperate and devoted that he ignored his friends, stopped looking for work, and ultimately gave up eating. Eventually, he died. When he found himself in front of God. He asked, "Lord, I prayed and believed in you with all my heart and might. My faith in you was unwavering. Why didn't you answer my prayer and make me wealthy?" To which God responded, "Well, you could've at least bought a lottery ticket."

So be mindful of your surroundings, but also be mindful with yourself.

To paraphrase *American History X,* someone else already said it best, so you may as well end with a quote. If you can't top it, steal it and go out strong. Since we began with a quote from Mark Twain it seems appropriate to end with one as well. Farewell, and remember:

"Twenty years from now you will be more disappointed by the things that you didn't do than by the ones you did do. So throw off the bowlines. Sail away from the safe harbor. Catch the trade winds in your sails. Explore. Dream. Discover."

ACKNOWLEDGMENTS

The only reason this book was possible is because of you, Iya. If it wasn't for all of your work, not only would this book not be anywhere near the level that it is, but it would likely live only on my hard drive, destined to never see the light of day. You are one of the most talented and incredible people that I know and I can't imagine what my life would have been if I didn't have you pushing me and supporting me in all my crazy endeavors. I couldn't have asked for a better sister than you. From the bottom of my heart and every cell in my body, thank you. [*Editor's Note*: We're all ridiculously proud of you. Love you, nerd.]

Thank you, Mom and Dad, for believing that I would finish, despite what your better judgment told you based on your past experiences. I don't know what I did in my last life to deserve parents like you but there is not a single day that I am not thankful that I have you to call family.

Christa, thank you for your patience, for putting up with me for the better part of the last year while I went headfirst down this rabbit hole. I know it could not have been easy to watch me yelling at my computer screen on a daily basis. You pushed me when I said there was no way I'd finish, and you comforted me when I doubted what I wrote. I love you.

Thank you to everyone who is in the book, and to everyone who isn't in the book but helped me research, review, or just listened to me complain or gloat about it. Thank you to anyone who is in or was in my life. No matter how long our relationship or how brief our meeting, I am the person that I am today because of all of you. For that I am eternally grateful.

A huge thank you to Eric, Brian, and everyone on the New Degree Press team. You helped me through each step of the way and talked me off the edge each time that I wanted to rage-quit. Hoya Saxa.

And lastly, thank you, reader. Let's meet again someday.

WORKS REFERENCED

———

Point of Departure

Ho, Leon. "How to Be Successful In Life? 13 Tips from the Most Successful People." *Lifehack*. October 30, 2018. https://www.lifehack.org/articles/lifestyle/how-to-be-successful-in-life.html.

Planning Your Trip

"Travel News, Airline Industry News, & Hotel Industry News by Skift." Skift. Accessed February 11, 2019. https://skift.com/.

Tom Lowry (Managing Editor for Skift), interviewed by George Megre, by telephone, January 11, 2019.

"New Study: Americans Say Road to Success Now Paved More with Fulfillment Than Wealth." American Express. May 15, 2013. https://about.americanexpress.com/press-release/new-study-americans-say-road-success-now-paved-more-fulfillment-wealth.

Jaaskelainen, Liisa. "Topic: Global Travel and Tourism Industry." Statista. Accessed February 11, 2019. https://www.statista.com/topics/962/global-tourism/.

"Travel & Tourism Economic Impact 2018 World." March 2018. https://www.wttc.org/-/media/files/reports/economic-impact-research/regions-2018/world2018.pdf.

Easterlin, Richard A. "Does Economic Growth Improve the Human Lot? Some Empirical Evidence." *Nations and Households in Economic Growth*, 1974, 89-125.

Jebb, Andrew T., Louis Tay, Ed Diener, and Shigehiro Oishi. "Happiness, Income Satiation and Turning Points Around the World." *Nature Human Behaviour* 2, no. 1 (2018): 33-38.

"Thomas D. Gilovich Talks About Human Behavior." Interview. *Masters In Business* (audio blog), January 25, 2018. https://soundcloud.com/bloombergview/thomas-d-gilovich-talks-about-human-behavior.

Carty, Meghan. "New Skift Research: U.S. Experiential Traveler Trends 2018." Skift. October 25, 2017. https://skift.com/2017/10/24/new-skift-research-u-s-experiential-traveler-trends-2018/.

Destination 1: Creativity

Crane, Brent. "For a More Creative Brain, Travel." *The Atlantic*. March 31, 2015. https://www.theatlantic.com/health/archive/2015/03/for-a-more-creative-brain-travel/388135/.

Novotney, Amy. "The Science of Creativity." American Psychological Association. *gradPSYCH*. January 2009. https://www.apa.org/gradpsych/2009/01/creativity.

Epstein, Robert, Steven M. Schmidt, and Regina Warfel. "Measuring and Training Creativity Competencies: Validation of a New Test." *Creativity Research Journal* 20, no. 1 (2008): 7-12.

"How to Make a Difference and Find Your Purpose — Blake Mycoskie (#249)." Interview. *The Tim Ferriss Show* (audio blog), June 28, 2017. https://tim.blog/tag/blake-mycoskie/.

Mycoskie, Blake. "How I Did It: The TOMS Story." *Entrepreneur*. September 20, 2011. https://www.entrepreneur.com/article/220350.

"The TOMS Story | TOMS®." TOMS® Official Site. Accessed February 11, 2019. https://www.toms.com/about-toms.

Buchanan, Leigh. "How Toms' Blake Mycoskie Built a $400 Million Business on Social Entrepreneurship." *Inc.* April 27, 2016. https://www.inc.com/magazine/201605/leigh-buchanan/toms-founder-blake-mycoskie-social-entrepreneurship.html.

"Energy Drink." Red Bull Can Lifecycle - Environment & Sustainability :: Energy Drink :: Red Bull USA. Accessed February 11, 2019. http://energydrink-us.redbull.com/en.

"Red Bull Founder." Red Bull Can Lifecycle - Environment & Sustainability :: Energy Drink :: Red Bull USA. Accessed February 11, 2019. https://energydrink-us.redbull.com/en/company.

Bhasin, Kim. "How Dietrich Mateschitz Ignored the Haters and Created the Top Energy Drink on the Planet." *Business Insider.* February 15, 2012. https://www.businessinsider.com/how-dietrich-mateschitz-ignored-the-haters-and-created-the-top-energy-drink-on-the-planet-2012-2#now-read-about-two-more-beverage-titans-14.

"Howard Schultz on Global Reach and Local Relevance at Starbucks." BCG. October 17, 2012. https://www.bcg.com/publications/2012/leadership-management-two-speed-economy-howard-schultz-global-reach-and-local-relevance.aspx.

"Company Information." Starbucks Coffee Company. Accessed February 11, 2019. https://www.starbucks.com/about-us/company-information.

Lebowitz, Shana. "From the Projects to a $2.3 Billion Fortune - the Inspiring Rags-to-riches Story of Starbucks CEO Howard Schultz." *Business Insider.* May 30, 2015. https://www.businessinsider.com/rags-to-riches-story-of-howard-schultz-2015-5.

Chuang, Tamara. "Report: Colorado's Home-grown Noosa Yoghurt Is for Sale Again." *The Denver Post.* January 12, 2018. https://www.denverpost.com/2018/01/11/colorado-noosa-yoghurt-for-sale/.

"Our Story | Leather Bags, Crochet Bags, Accessories." The Sak. Accessed February 11, 2019. https://www.thesak.com/pages/our-story.

TEDx Talks. "How adventure makes you smarter, stronger, and attractive: Tyler Tervooren at TEDxConcordiaUPortland." YouTube. May 08, 2014. https://www.youtube.com/watch?v=-2S7Iz38ZDik.

Godart, Frédéric C., William W. Maddux, Andrew V. Shipilov, and Adam D. Galinsky. "Fashion with a Foreign Flair: Professional Experiences Abroad Facilitate the Creative Innovations of Organizations." *Academy of Management Journal* 58, no. 1 (2015): 195-220.

Maddux, William W., and Adam D. Galinsky. "Cultural Borders and Mental Barriers: The Relationship between Living Abroad and Creativity." *Journal of Personality and Social Psychology* 96, no. 5 (2009): 1047-061.

Destination 2: Perspective

Charitywater. "The Spring – The Charity: Water Story." YouTube. August 29, 2016. https://www.youtube.com/watch?v=UE9U-vT5ujyg.

INBOUND. "Scott Harrison | INBOUND 2018 Keynote." YouTube. September 07, 2018. https://www.youtube.com/watch?-time_continue=5&v=V4E1t2yIZlc.

"To Scale, You Must Master the Art of Storytelling." Interview. *Masters of Scale* (audio blog), December 18, 2018. https://mastersofscale.com/scott-harrison-to-scale-you-must-master-the-art-of-storytelling/.

"Mercy Ships | Who We Are." Mercy Ships. Accessed February 11, 2019. https://www.mercyships.org/who-we-are/.

Wolfe, Alexandra. "Scott Harrison Turned From Nightclub Promoter to Philanthropist." *The Wall Street Journal*. September 14, 2018. https://www.wsj.com/articles/scott-harrison-turned-from-nightclub-promoter-to-philanthropist-1536949475.

Nicholas Erardi (Consultant for Accenture), interviewed by George Megre, New York, NY, July 29, 2018.

Ari Gordon (Co-founder and COO for SagePlate), interviewed by George Megre, by telephone, November 9, 2018.

Harris, Sam. *Free Will*. London: Simon & Schuster, 2012.

Adam, Hajo, Otilia Obodaru, Jackson G. Lu, William W. Maddux, and Adam D. Galinsky. "The Shortest Path to Oneself Leads around the World: Living Abroad Increases Self-concept Clarity." *Organizational Behavior and Human Decision Processes* 145 (2018): 16-29.

Destination 3: Confidence

TEDx Talks. "Confidence: What Does It Do? | Richard Petty | TEDxOhioStateUniversity." YouTube. March 16, 2015. https://www.youtube.com/watch?v=cKu-32iyHso.

Michael Sobalvarro (Translation Science Research Intern for Georgetown University), interviewed by George Megre, by telephone, November 12, 2018.

"Resolving Health and Economic Disparities." Global Brigades. Accessed February 11, 2019. https://www.globalbrigades.org/about-us/vision-mission/.

Leith, William. "Is Tegucigalpa the Crime Capital of the World?" *The Spectator.* February 24, 2018. https://www.spectator.co.uk/2018/02/is-tegucigalpa-the-crime-capital-of-the-world/.

Jessica Rohrer (Portfolio Manager for Pathway Lending), interviewed by George Megre, by telephone, November 15, 2018.

ZeitgeistMinds. "Malcolm Gladwell - Zeitgeist Americas 2013." YouTube. September 16, 2013. https://www.youtube.com/watch?v=3UEwbRWFZVc.

Hartmans, Avery. "The Fabulous Life of Airbnb's Brian Chesky, One of the Youngest and Richest Tech Founders in America." *Business Insider.* July 22, 2017. https://www.businessinsider.com/brian-chesky-airbnb-ceo-life-story-photos-2017-7#along-with-a-third-cofounder-nathan-blecharczyk-gebbia-and-chesky-started-what-was-at-the-time-called-airbedandbreakfast-com-8.

Brown, Paul B. "'You Miss 100% Of The Shots You Don't Take.' You Need To Start Shooting At Your Goals." *Forbes*. January 12, 2014. https://www.forbes.com/sites/actiontrumpsevery-thing/2014/01/12/you-miss-100-of-the-shots-you-dont-take-so-start-shooting-at-your-goal/#6a8f3of86a40.

Lewis, Gregory. "Chisholm Was Beacon of Hope to a Generation." *Sun-Sentinel*. September 26, 2018. https://www.sun-sentinel.com/news/fl-xpm-2005-01-04-0501040175-story.html.

Visionaryproject. "Shirley Chisholm : Growing Up in Barbados." YouTube. April 26, 2010. https://www.youtube.com/watch?v=I1ZPJ2eSzAY.

Destination 4: New Skills

Harline, Craig. "Five to Nine Things You Maybe Didn't Know About Mormon Missionaries." *The Huffington Post*. November 23, 2014. https://www.huffingtonpost.com/craig-harline/mormon-missionaries-_b_5869448.html.

Vincent Liew (Global Executive Director for Boldface Hospitality), interviewed by George Megre, by telephone, November 11, 2018.

Jerry Wang (Principal for The Carlyle Group), interviewed by George Megre, by telephone, December 17, 2018.

Colin Deffet (International Sales for Allied Mineral Products), interviewed by George Megre, by telephone, November 2, 2018.

"History." Peace Corps. Accessed February 11, 2019. https://www.peacecorps.gov/about/history/.

Capture Your Flag. "Simon Sinek: Why Travel to Distant and Unfamiliar Places." YouTube. November 28, 2012. https://www.youtube.com/watch?v=4bepgUdZHok.

Pearce, Philip L., and Faith Foster. "A "University of Travel": Backpacker Learning." *Tourism Management* 28, no. 5 (2007): 1285-298.

Destination 5: Wellness

"Vacations and Your Heart." Cleveland HeartLab, Inc. Accessed February 11, 2019. http://www.clevelandheartlab.com/blog/vacations-and-your-heart/.

Gump, Brooks B., and Karen A. Matthews. "Are Vacations Good for Your Health? The 9-Year Mortality Experience After the Multiple Risk Factor Intervention Trial." *Psychosomatic Medicine* 62, no. 5 (2000): 608-12.

Eaker, Elaine D., Joan Pinsky, and William P. Castelli. "Myocardial Infarction and Coronary Death among Women: Psychosocial

Predictors from a 20-Year Follow-up of Women in the Framingham Study." *American Journal of Epidemiology* 135, no. 8 (1992): 854-64.

Ferriss, Timothy. *The 4-hour Workweek: Escape 9-5, Live Anywhere, and Join the New Rich*. New York: Harmony Books, 2012.

Greater Good Science Center. "Richard Davidson: The Four Constituents of Well-Being." YouTube. January 28, 2016. https://www.youtube.com/watch?v=HeBpsiFQiTI.

Davidson, Richard. "The Four Keys to Well-Being." *Greater Good Magazine*. March 21, 2016. https://greatergood.berkeley.edu/article/item/the_four_keys_to_well_being.

"'Wellness Tourism' Is Fastest Growing Travel Sector, Says Lonely Planet." Eye for Travel. January 2, 2018. https://www.eyefor-travel.com/distribution-strategies/wellness-tourism-fastest-growing-travel-sector-says-lonely-planet.

Meyer, Robinson. "In the Brain, Memories Are Inextricably Tied to Place." *The Atlantic*. August 13, 2014. https://www.theatlantic.com/technology/archive/2014/08/in-the-brain-memories-are-inextricably-tied-to-place/375969/.

Destination 6: Network

Julia – (Consultant), interviewed by George Megre, by telephone, January 6, 2019.

Priscilla Babb, interviewed by George Megre, New York, NY, January 9, 2019.

Ryan, Andrew. "Bill Murray Crashes Bachelor Party, Gives Marriage Advice." *The Globe and Mail.* May 12, 2018. https://www.theglobeandmail.com/life/celebrity-news/the-a-list/bill-murray-crashes-bachelor-party-gives-marriage-advice/article18880697/.

Barshad, Amos. "Bill Murray's Latest Role: Part-Time Bartender." *Vulture.* March 24, 2010. https://www.vulture.com/2010/03/bill_murrays_latest_role_part.html.

Cao, Jiyin, Adam D. Galinsky, and William W. Maddux. "Does Travel Broaden the Mind? Breadth of Foreign Experiences Increases Generalized Trust." *Social Psychological and Personality Science* 5, no. 5 (2013): 517-25.

Jackson, Chris, and Negar Ballard. "Over Half of Americans Report Feeling Like No One Knows Them Well." Ipsos. May 1, 2018. https://www.ipsos.com/en-us/news-polls/us-loneliness-index-report.

Thayer, Colette, and G. Oscar Anderson. "Loneliness and Social Connections: A National Survey of Adults 45 and Older." *AARP Research*. September 2018.

Apperson, Joyce. "Chronic Loneliness - Could It Be a Silent Killer?" Caring Connection, Inc. September 21, 2018. https://www.caringconnectionmd.com/blog/chronic-loneliness/.

Destination 7: Spirituality

Fred Rooney (Fulbright Scholar), interviewed by George Megre, by telephone, December 12, 2019.

Rashid, Brian. "Fred Rooney: Affording Legal Justice to All." *Forbes*. November 16, 2015. https://www.forbes.com/sites/brianrashid/2015/11/15/how-fred-rooney-is-democratizing-affordable-access-to-legal-justice-worldwide/#81684656f5b5.

Biswas, Rounak. "Fred Rooney, Attorney-at-Law, on Being Fulbright Specialist and Global Advocate for Justice." SuperLawyer. May 25, 2017. https://superlawyer.in/fred-rooney-attorney-at-law-fulbright-specialist-global-advocate-for-justice/

Brian Rashid (CEO for Brian Rashid Global), interviewed by George Megre, New York, NY, January 7, 2019.

Kozinn, Allan. "George Harrison, Former Beatle, Dies at 58." *The New York Times*. November 30, 2001. https://www.nytimes.com/2001/11/30/obituaries/george-harrison-former-beatle-dies-at-58.html.

"George Harrison." Biography.com. April 28, 2017. https://www.biography.com/people/george-harrison-9206804.

Slate, Jeff. "Why George Harrison Has Become the Most Popular Beatle." NBC News. February 25, 2018. https://www.nbcnews.com/think/opinion/george-harrison-75-how-quietest-beatle-became-most-popular-one-ncna850986.

"George Harrison Quotes." BrainyQuote. Accessed February 11, 2019. https://www.brainyquote.com/quotes/george_harrison_177108.

Runtagh, Jordan. "Hear the Beatles' Last-Ever Concert." *Rolling Stone*. June 25, 2018. https://www.rollingstone.com/music/music-features/remembering-beatles-final-concert-247497/.

Frost, Caroline. "George Harrison Died 15 Years Ago Today: We Remember The Quiet Beatle's Most Inspiring Quotes." *The Huffington Post*. November 29, 2016. https://www.huffingtonpost.co.uk/entry/george-harrison-quotes_uk_583c-3b5ee4b0207d1918b650.

Cosgrove, Ben. "Concert for Bangladesh: Photos From the First-Ever Benefit Rock Show." *Time*. July 30, 2013. http://time.com/3877705/concert-for-bangladesh-photos-from-the-first-ever-benefit-rock-show/.

"The Spirit of George Harrison." Beatlesnumber9. Accessed February 11, 2019. http://beatlesnumber9.com/george.html.

Gupta, Sahil Mohan. "What Steve Jobs Did in India 35 Years Ago." Gadgets 360. June 06, 2012. https://gadgets.ndtv.com/others/news/what-steve-jobs-did-in-india-35-years-ago-225246.

"What Really Shaped Steve Jobs' View of India - Realms of Intuition or the Pains of Delhi Belly?" *The Economic Times*. October 25, 2011. https://economictimes.indiatimes.com/what-really-shaped-steve-jobs-view-of-india-realms-of-intuition-or-the-pains-of-delhi-belly/articleshow/10480591.cms.

"Narendra Modi & Mark Zuckerberg at Facebook HQ | Townhall Q&A | San Jose." Dailymotion. December 21, 2015. https://www.dailymotion.com/video/x3itatb.

Destination 8: Study

"Global Immersion Program." Columbia Business School. October 31, 2018. https://www8.gsb.columbia.edu/chazen/students/globalimmersion.

"International Consulting Projects." McDonough School of Business | Georgetown University. Accessed February 11, 2019. https://msb.georgetown.edu/global-business-initiative/international-consulting-projects.

"The Field Method." Harvard Business School. Accessed February 11, 2019. https://www.hbs.edu/mba/academic-experience/Pages/the-field-method.aspx.

Bryon Grigsby (President of Moravian College), interviewed by George Megre, by telephone, January 2, 2019.

Nevadomski Berdan, Stacie. "Study Abroad Numbers Up Again-But What About Foreign Language as Part of the Experience?" *The Huffington Post.* November 15, 2017. https://www.huffingtonpost.com/entry/study-abroad-numbers-up-againbut-what-about-foreign_us_5a0cb662e4b023a796fed38f.

"College History." Moravian College. Accessed February 11, 2019. https://www.moravian.edu/about/college-history.

"View of the World: Global Education, Global Impact." *Moravian College Magazine,* Fall 2018. http://read.nxtbook.com/moravian_college/moravian_college_magazine/fall_2018/view_of_the_world.html

"Economic Diversity and Student Outcomes at Moravian." *The New York Times.* January 18, 2017. https://www.nytimes.com/interactive/projects/college-mobility/moravian-college.

"Economic Diversity and Student Outcomes at Penn." *The New York Times.* January 18, 2017. https://www.nytimes.com/interactive/projects/college-mobility/university-of-pennsylvania.

McCarthy, Niall. "The Share Of Americans Holding A Passport Has Increased Dramatically In Recent Years [Infographic]." *Forbes.* January 11, 2018. https://www.forbes.com/sites/niallmccarthy/2018/01/11/the-share-of-americans-holding-a-passport-has-increased-dramatically-in-recent-years-infographic/#7668a1283c16.

Pantelis Colakis (Business Development for DrumWave), interviewed by George Megre, New York, NY, November 7, 2018.

Sood, Suemedha. "Travel - The Statistics of Studying Abroad." *BBC News.* September 26, 2012. http://www.bbc.com/travel/story/20120926-the-statistics-of-studying-abroad.

Redden, Elizabeth. "Study Abroad Numbers Grow." Inside Higher Ed. November 13, 2018. https://www.insidehighered.com/news/2018/11/13/study-abroad-numbers-continue-grow-driven-continued-growth-short-term-programs.

"Trends in U.S. Study Abroad." NAFSA. Accessed February 11, 2019. https://www.nafsa.org/Policy_and_Advocacy/Policy_Resources/Policy_Trends_and_Data/Trends_in_U_S__Study_Abroad/.

"What Statistics Show about Study Abroad Students." Study Abroad. Accessed February 11, 2019. https://studyabroad.ucmerced.edu/study-abroad-statistics/statistics-study-abroad#resources.

"Benefits of Study Abroad." IES Abroad. July 25, 2018. https://www.iesabroad.org/study-abroad/benefits.

"Alumni Survey Results." IES Abroad. January 11, 2018. https://www.iesabroad.org/study-abroad/benefits/alumni-survey-results.

Preston, Kendra. "Recent Graduates Survey: The Impact of Studying Abroad on Recent College Graduates' Careers: 2006-2011 Graduates." IES Abroad Recent Graduate Survey. May 2012. https://www.iesabroad.org/system/files/resources/recentgraduatessurvey_0.pdf.

"AIFS Study Abroad Outcomes." American Institute for Foreign Study. Accessed February 11, 2019. https://www.aifsabroad.com/advisors/pdf/AIFS_Study_Abroad_Outcomes.pdf.

"Paul Simon Study Abroad Act Back on Legislative Cards." *University World News.* November 18, 2017. https://www.universityworldnews.com/post.php?story=20171118065110166.

"Should I Take Time Off?" Harvard College. Accessed February 11, 2019. https://college.harvard.edu/admissions/preparing-college/should-i-take-time.

Skiba, Katherine. "Malia Obama's Gap Year about to End as She Goes to Harvard." *Chicago Tribune.* August 18, 2017. https://www.chicagotribune.com/news/local/politics/ct-malia-obama-starts-harvard-met-0818-20170818-story.html.

Hoe, Nina. "American Gap Association National Alumni Survey: Report." American Gap Association, Temple University. Accessed February 11, 2019. http://www.americangap.org/assets/2015 NAS Report.pdf.

"Gap Year Data & Benefits." Gap Year Association. Accessed February 11, 2019. https://www.gapyearassociation.org/data-benefits.php.

"Optimism for Student Voter Turnout." Inside Higher Ed. Accessed February 11, 2019. https://www.insidehighered.com/news/2018/08/14/advocacy-groups-expect-uptick-college-student-voter-turnout.

Destination 9: Work

Gallagher, Colleen. "GBTA Forecasts Seven Percent Growth in Global Business Travel Spend, Potentially Signifying End to Era of Uncertainty." The Global Business Travel Association. August 14, 2018. https://www.gbta.org/news-and-advocacy/newsroom/gbta-forecasts-seven-percent-growth-in-global-business-travel-spend-potentially-signifying-end-to-era-of-uncertainty.

"Singapore Airlines Launches World's Longest Flight." Singapore Airlines. October 12, 2018. https://www.singaporeair.com/en_UK/us/media-centre/press-release/article/?q=en_UK/2018/October-December/ne3418-181012.

"Paul English on Lola's Debut for Business Travelers." *Business Travel News*. October 04, 2017. https://www.businesstravelnews.com/Interviews/Paul-English-on-Lolas-Debut-for-Business-Travelers-Today.

Jason Gershenson (Attorney for White Summers Caffee & James, LLP), interviewed by George Megre, New York, NY, January 4, 2019.

Lillian – (Consultant for BCG), interviewed by George Megre, New York, NY, December 14, 2018.

Kalil Nicolas (Senior Associate, Corporate and Investment Banking for Citi), interviewed by George Megre, by telephone, September 17, 2018.

"2018 Alternative Workplace Strategies Fifth Biennial Benchmarking Study." Global Workplace Analytics. Accessed February 11, 2019. https://globalworkplaceanalytics.com/telecommuting-statistics.

Bresiger, Gregory. "This Is How Much Time Employees Spend Slacking off." *New York Post*. July 30, 2017. https://nypost.com/2017/07/29/this-is-how-much-time-employees-spend-slacking-off/.

"Costs and Benefits – Global Workplace Analytics." Global Workplace Analytics. Accessed February 11, 2019. https://globalworkplaceanalytics.com/resources/costs-benefits.

"Expat Life - What Are the Financial and Lifestyle Benefits?" Expat Network. March 01, 2018. https://www.expatnetwork.com/financial-lifestyle-benefits-expat-life/.

Jet, Johnny. "Are Bleisure Trips Becoming More Common? This Study Says Yes." *Forbes*. October 25, 2018. https://www.forbes.com/sites/johnnyjet/2018/10/25/are-bleisure-trips-becoming-more-common-this-study-says-yes/#131a6c1c75ed.

Destination 10: Leisure

"State of American Vacation 2018." Project: Time Off. September 18, 2018. https://projecttimeoff.com/reports/state-of-american-vacation-2018/.

Frye, Lisa. "More People Are Taking Time Off, and That's Good for Business." Society for Human Resource Management. June 01, 2018. https://www.shrm.org/resourcesandtools/hr-topics/employee-relations/pages/workers-taking-more-vacation-.aspx.

"State of American Vacation 2018." Project: Time Off. Accessed February 11, 2019. https://projecttimeoff.com/wp-content/uploads/2018/05/StateofAmericanVacation2018.pdf.

"Solo Travel Statistics and Data : 2018 - 2019." Solo Traveler. Accessed February 11, 2019. https://solotravelerworld.com/about/solo-travel-statistics-data/.

TEDx Talks. "The real reason I traveled to 196 countries | Cassie De Pecol | TEDxMileHigh." YouTube. August 25, 2017. https://www.youtube.com/watch?v=gMM-mr4CTYo.

Destination 11: At Home

Lu, Jackson G., Andrew C. Hafenbrack, Paul W. Eastwick, Dan J. Wang, William W. Maddux, and Adam D. Galinsky. "'Going

Out' of the Box: Close Intercultural Friendships and Romantic Relationships Spark Creativity, Workplace Innovation, and Entrepreneurship." *Journal of Applied Psychology* 102, no. 7 (2017): 1091-108.

Gallen, Joel. *Ellen DeGeneres: Here and Now.* HBO, 2003.

Stöppler, Melissa Conrad. "Meditation May Reduce Stress and Improves Health by MedicineNet.com." MedicineNet. June 13, 2018. https://www.medicinenet.com/stress_meditation_may_reduce_stress/views.htm.

Campbell, Denis. "Walking a Mile a Day Can Cut Risk of Dying from Cancer by 40% – Study." *The Guardian.* August 28, 2014. https://www.theguardian.com/society/2014/aug/29/walking-mile-day-cut-risk-dying-breast-prostate-cancer-40pc.

Spiegel, Alix, and Micaela Rodríguez. "Eager To Burst His Own Bubble, A Techie Made Apps To Randomize His Life." NPR. June 08, 2017. https://www.npr.org/sections/alltechconsidered/2017/06/08/531796329/eager-to-burst-his-own-bubble-a-techie-made-apps-to-randomize-his-life.

Made in the USA
Middletown, DE
16 May 2019